HOW TO TALK TO BOYS

Dianne Todaro

ALLEN&UNWIN

Contents

To Carla and Luke.
To thy own self be true.

About the author

Dianne Todaro is passionate about children's education and creating books that engage communication between parents, teachers and the child. She believes the best gift we can give a child is the ability to articulate what they need to be nourished in their everyday life.

After becoming a primary school teacher, her career path over the past 20 years has evolved to include a range of book projects that promote her passion for commercial and educational value on issues that benchmark the hallmarks of being an everyday kid. Her recent concepts *Puberty Girl* and *Puberty Boy* are now translated in 10 countries worldwide.

Dianne recently restructured Interrelate Family Centres, the school services division. Her role as the coordinator of all school programs charged her with the responsibility for providing leadership to a team of educators who teach sexuality and relationship education to 30,000 parents and children per year.

Dianne is the director of her own company, communicate kids. Visit www.communicatekids.com for more information.

Acknowledgements

A big bunch of loving thanks sprinkled with memorable moments that have certainly helped me to be the girl (woman) I am today:

How lucky am I to have my own daughter on the front cover of my book and have my son help with the artwork. Yes, I can believe it! They are both articulate and incredible kids who I love very much. My cousin Liz Seymour, who continually waves her magic wand over all my ideas. The best chick publisher Annette Barlow for your appreciation in the educational value of my book concepts, and editor Christa Munns for keeping me on track and on time. To Dr Jonathan Toussaint author of *How To Talk to Girls*, what an honor to have our books stand next to each other in the bookshops—can't wait to start talking to teens with you! Davey Mac (also known as Teazer) for his brilliant street art on the cover. Katrina Crook for her epic cover shot. Miss Moira Loader and her fantabulous 2010 Year 10 Religion Class at Our Lady of Mercy College, Burraneer (which by the way is the school I actually went to @ 12 years of age, OMG!). Miss Margaret King, Head Welfare teacher at Cabramatta High

School—you rock! Thanks for coordinating a vibrant, young and diverse group of girls to talk about boys. (We could have talked for hours. In fact I think we did!) Dr Dasia Black for your quote and inspiration on child development that I have carried with me my entire professional life. Domino Grice Wilson for assisting me in my initial research and Jacqueline Jayne King, Fern Christian, Kristen Hedgepeth for sharing their wisdom, strength and experience on talking to boys. Kisses to my very own six-pack of friends: Jo Thyer, Lynne Gullifa, Glenice Bland, Roxanne Young, Debbie Cockburn and Jane Nash. To the women who have helped shape me to be the girl I am today, I do not have the words to express my love for each of you: Matron Jean Watson, Diane Young, my sister Jennifer Anne Pinker and my mum Barbara May Wells (may she rest in peace 18/2/2010). Respectful thanks to all the boys I have talked with throughout my life (including my dad Alan John Wells and brothers Peter and Daryl) and, finally, a special note of gratitude to the boys and men I talked with while actually writing *How to Talk to Boys*. Thank god for boys, this world just wouldn't be the same without them in it. Hey girls!

Introduction

Wow, this is a big responsibility to write a book on how girls talk to boys—I must be some expert on this me-girl you-boy thing. But really I am just a normal girl (woman) like you. I was in your place once and had many, many talking-to-boys experiences, starting from as young as 12—some good, some great, some not so good, and some really bad. Oh yes, I fell for the 'hottie'—the bad boy. And it took me till the age of 21 to get back on track with my life and work out my dreams and goals, and how I would start again to learn how to talk to boys with respect and dignity in my heart.

Along the way I became a teacher, a mum, an ideas person for books and an author. I eventually met the man I would marry, in a kitchen washing dishes—he called me Sam girl and I called him Sam boy. We started out as really good friends, and that love and respect for each other grew—but even the most strengthened hearts can crumble over time if you stop talking.

Lucky how life sometimes gives you another chance and brings you back around full circle ... I finally got the lessons on how to be true to myself and how to talk to boys, and now so do you! Very bold, flirtatious, awkward, painful, memorable and fun talking times with boys are definitely ahead of you. And, yes, the boy–girl talking thing will alert emotions you never thought you had—especially when you're talking to those 'hotties' who can turn your best thinking into gush!

I talk to girls of all ages every day about how they talk to boys (especially the texting) and we all agree on one thing: 'It can get very complicated.' How girls talk to boys is not rocket science. But there is actually a bit of method to this sophisticated world of 'communication' we are all living in today, and the more prepared we are in the way we connect, the more present we will be speaking to that boy one-to-one.

You will find that *How to Talk to Boys* leaves nothing unsaid, unpacks all the so-called girl–boy rules, and even attempts to entertain the thought that we can meet our prince if we let him come and find us! It seems too simple that if you just get on with your own life and do the things you love and that make you passionate, then you will be very attractive, especially to that one special boy who wants to get to know you.

In this book you'll explore how boys tick, tock and what they actually talk about.

1
Talking about talking

Inside each of us are the answers to all life's tricky questions, especially the one about how we talk to boys. But just like anything we do, the more we practise it the better we become. Talking to boys can be quite different to talking to girls, and I warn that for some of you it may take a little time before you feel totally comfortable, especially if you have a physical reaction to that particular boy who is very cute. I like to call it that 'gushy' feeling you have when you see him and all 'smart chick thinking' ideals somehow fly out the window. Oh boys, the mystery of those good looking, smart, cheeky monkeys! It would be impossible to live without boys, but it can sometimes feel like it is impossible to get to talk to them, too. So let's ignore all impossibilities and explore all the possibilities in how us girls communicate with boys.

Here's what teenage girls (ages 12–17) from two Sydney high schools thought talking (communicating) to boys would actually involve:

'Successful communication means being able to get your intended message across to the other person. Sharing thoughts. Chatting. MSN. Facebook. Phoning. Being confident. Connecting and making a bond. Vocally talking to him. A lot of talking and listening.

Communication with boys is …'Friendly, flirty, happy, open, confident, sometimes sarcastic! Boys are fun. I'm not shy of boys, and can be myself. Sometimes boys don't realise some things they say are rude.'
—Ruby, age 15
'I find that boys are less open about feelings.'
—Lisa, age 15

Socialising, connecting and understanding where the other person is coming from.'

When it comes to talking to boys, especially that boy who takes your breath away, it is definitely a good idea to be able to get in touch with your truest feelings, and be honest and open with yourself about what you are experiencing when that boy starts talking to you. Will he be a boy who will just remain your friend or is he the boy who will make your heart and head go 'zing'?

How do you know? Knowing how we all talk and the impact of how we come across to the world in general is certainly an excellent place to start to unlock any uncertainties you may have in moving towards a respectful relationship with talking to boys!

Experts on talking

The way that most of us have actually learnt to communicate—that is, exchange our ideas, deal with arguments, express our thoughts, let the world know what we believe, stand up for ourselves and put our truest feelings on the line—is from our parents, or those adults who have raised us and have had the most influence over our first 12 years of life. I call these years the 'marshmallow years', the soft and gooey years where we just soak up everything before we set down to be the girl we are going to be in our teenage years.

Just like learning to walk, we have all learnt to talk. Our parents are there to hear our first words, but when it comes to talking to boys they are not going to be there holding our hands (thank God!) Parents teach us to talk—not just through their words but also through their actions—and this actually does have a major influence on the way we relate to boys.

A major influence in my studies of communication between parents and children was my university senior lecturer in child development, Dr Dasia Black. I quote her because I believe in her understanding of what a child needs in order to develop into that girl who will want to connect with that boy when he finds her.

'In order to thrive children need to experience the permanence, continuity, commitment of known, loved and loving adults, providers of nutrition, stimulation, loving touch, responsive care and secure attachment. Responsive care is the most challenging task for parents it requires parent to "read" the child accurately in order to respond to his/her thoughts and feelings rather than those in the parents' head. Parents need to set aside their preconceived notions and listen to what the child has to say, in words and/or body language; to attempt to step into the child's shoes and see their point of view and then to communicate their understanding of the child in a language the child can understand. Effective communication with children models for them the key element of rewarding relationships'.

Our childhood years frame us. They set us up for how we will talk and 'do' relationships in our teen and later adult years. These years demonstrate to us the possibilities to love and be loved in relationships. If these experiences are not there, some of us will go searching for love in all the wrong places until we are able to stop and find the capacity to seek out healthy role models who show us unconditional love and the ability to self care and love ourselves first.

Intellectual talk

Our intelligence (brains trust) is capable of being massaged like a muscle. Give it regular exercise and it will work even better. That means our ability to learn more information about talking to boys can improve the way we actually do it. But talking to boys is not like getting ready for a maths exam, where once you have got the formula it will keep working repeatedly. Like anything, it takes practice, and some of you will have a natural ability to do it, whereas others will struggle. The important factor here is to know where you are on the line between finding it 'easy talking to boys' and 'really difficult to even think about talking to boys'.

Generally girls tend to talk through a lot of detail, whereas boys seem to be more straightforward, speaking in short sentences and not giving a lot away, except when we ask the right type of open-ended question that can bring out the little boy in the big boy you are talking to. Watch his eyes light up as his memories tell you more about the boy he is today.

Emotional talk

We communicate emotionally when we express our feelings. Articulating our feelings can be quite difficult for some of us, especially if our EQ (emotional intelligence) is limited or we are not used to people asking us how we feel. A lot of songs we listen to are artists expressing their feelings, especially about girls talking to boys and vice versa.

Girls tend to identify their feelings more easily than boys. Why? It will depend on how you have grown up as a child and whether or not you have built up an emotional vocabulary (that is, whether you can identify feelings other than 'good' and 'bad', which are not actually feelings anyway). Ask that boy how he feels today, and see what type of response you get—probably 'tired' will be a big one, because those boys are using a lot of energy to grow physically, especially between the ages of 12 and 16.

One day in the not so distant future, EQ will become more important than IQ. Teenage boys today are more aware of the need to talk about their feelings and are using extra tools like electronic feeling faces to express themselves. This can only be a great thing! If boys are tracking their way to talking to girls and understanding how they feel when they see them, the more words they have in the EQ department to express their true feelings, the easier talking will be.

Illustration: Sam Young from *Puberty Boy*

'A teenager's hairstyle may be their only personal signature that shows the outside world how they feel inside.'

Social talk

We communicate socially by the friends we choose and the places we go, as well as through the values we display, which are often determined by those that our families demonstrated to us in our early years.

Bad boys, good boys, fun boys, nerds, surfs, technos, tech heads, graph artists—there are all types of boys, just as there are all types of girls, too. The families we grow up in, the sports we participate in, and a whole range of cultural, religious and financial factors will determine what type of social group you will end up in, but the one thing that is common to everyone is that girls will talk to boys from all walks of life, and vice versa.

Make it fun and try not to be too judgemental when you first get to know a new boy. Give him a chance as he may be very kind, generous and loving under that 'daggy' black hoody he never takes off!

Spiritual talk

We all communicate spiritually. Each of us has our own unique value system, set of beliefs and religion (or lack thereof) that

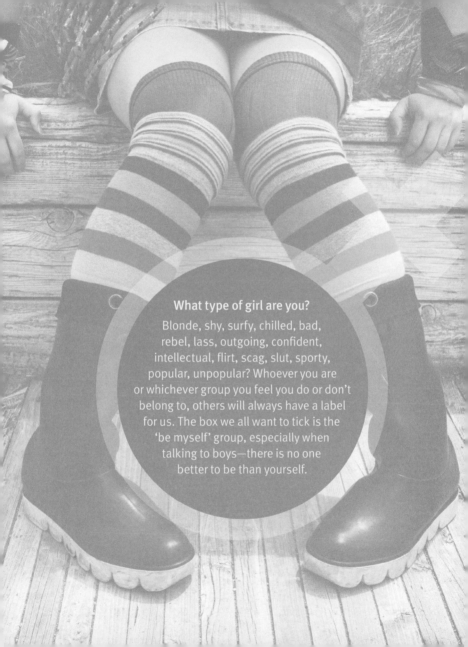

What type of girl are you?

Blonde, shy, surfy, chilled, bad, rebel, lass, outgoing, confident, intellectual, flirt, scag, slut, sporty, popular, unpopular? Whoever you are or whichever group you feel you do or don't belong to, others will always have a label for us. The box we all want to tick is the 'be myself' group, especially when talking to boys—there is no one better to be than yourself.

we use to steer ourselves in everyday decisions. Knowing how to make a decision that is right for you is having the ability to connect with your intuition, your gut feeling and your instinct. We all have an inbuilt conscience that guides us to know what is in our own best interest; it's up to us to get in touch with it and to decide whether or not to listen.

Stop and sit still to listen to yourself. Give yourself space to find out if this boy feels right for you? Talk to a friend you respect if you still can't work it out and then sit still again and come to your own conclusion.

Creative talk

We also communicate creatively. This I like to view as adding our very own individuality to the way we get our messages across, a little like how each of our signatures have their own creative flair. Based on years of practice, our signature may change from how it looks when we are 12 to when we sign our first driver's licence, and this is very similar to how it is with talking to boys. The more you talk to boys, the better you get at it and the more experienced you will become in knowing how they respond to the way you talk to them. If no one can understand your signature you tweak it a bit so it is readable. I am not saying we have to tweak ourselves and change to suit boys, but we can always improve our communication skills to achieve whatever it is we're after. Knowing the way you 'talk' and what your own personal expectations are when that boy starts talking to you are some of the first things you need to be conscious about. Ask yourself, do you really want to talk to this boy?

Do we talk scientifically to boys?

Your pheromones (sensory sniff bombs) are launching off their rocket pads. And our sensory sniff bombs can naturally decode these translucent chemicals floating around our bodies. They are our built-in natural sexual attraction to boys. You can't see them, but they are actually very real particles that can only be picked up by our sense of smell. They give you that 'gushy' feeling inside that tells you that you just can't wait to see that boy.

So the answer to the question is 'yes', there is such a thing as talking scientifically to boys, by using our sensory systems. Some of you may have experienced that 'zing' feeling in your body when a particular boy you like walks into your radar. It can be an overwhelming feeling right through your body, which makes you know in your 'gut' that you want to get to know this boy. You might think it could just be the way he looks, but then why doesn't this feeling go off with every boy you see? This can become really confusing, especially if your parents have told you that you are too young to be talking to boys, or you don't want to get distracted talking to boys because you are trying to focus on your study or extracurricular activities like dance, swimming or music.

Sexual attraction

Our sexuality is a way of talking too! That is, the way our bodies and our thinking combine to tell us we are ready to start talking to boys. Over the years we change from little girl thinking to young teen thinking, to thinking as a young woman, and so on. Our physical changes in puberty that 'no one escapes'— pimply moments, new hair in all those extra-sensitive spots like the pubic area and underarms, girls getting breasts, and boys' chests widening and voices deepening—are the outward signs that we are changing into young men and women. But the most incredible change is that our bodies are now capable of procreating. Yes, that's right—making babies! Puberty marks the time when you girls now have half the information to make a baby and boys the other half. Just incredible science, and with that comes the SHEBANG!—sexual attraction—an entirely new way of combining your thinking and talking when you feel a natural urge that we might call the 'zing' in your body that can be stirred up by a particular boy that your body is naturally attracted to. Unfortunately your body will not recognise whether or not that boy has the same thinking you have about culture, family values and beliefs. That places a big onus on you to get to know that boy.

Physical attraction

Today, we have become so sophisticated in the way we communicate through the use of language in words, numbers and symbols that our sense of smell is less relied on than our sense of sight. Our visual world, our first impression of what we see, is the most common way for us to be guided to make a choice today on what boy we want to talk to and get to know. Some girls call boys 'eye candy', and while some boys can't wait for girls to come into the 'candy shop' and talk to them, others may wish they would stop staring. It will take time to find your own level of confidence to judge which boys you feel physically attracted to talk to and want to get to know.

We communicate physically—with our body, our hands, what we wear—as well as through the actual words that come from our mouths; the way we choose to express them and also the words we choose to leave out. Some of us can even sing! Others get 'tongue tied'; you may have heard of this expression, meaning you just can't get out in words what is on your mind. This can often happen when talking to boys, but it can also happen when we are troubled by our thoughts and worried about what other people might think of us if we speak our truth, our mind.

I would love to tell you, girls, that there is an exact recipe to follow to talk to boys and you will all end up with the perfect sponge cake, all fluffy and yummy, ready to eat, but I am afraid that talking to boys is not that simple. The way you speak, smile, giggle and shy away, and the way you put your total package of attraction together is unique to you. The key is to know how you come across to the world of boys, and be confident and happy in yourself in the way you do your thang.

2

The 'me girl,
you boy'
thang!

What do boys talk about?

At the risk of generalising, boys like talking about the things they have accomplished, like winning their game of sport on the weekend or how the team they barrack for won the season. Or how cool a piece of street art is on some wall and if they know the artist who painted it, or how they might get to go to an event where they can see their favourite band. You girls, on the other hand, like talking about the relationships you have with the other people going to see the band, who you know that is going, how you will all get there, and, of course, what you are going to wear.

It's not that us girls are not proud of the things we achieve, like winning the netball competition, or getting an award at school for academic achievement or four years' work as a library monitor, but it's not generally the first thing we will put forward about ourselves on our homepage to show boys who we are. However, if there is a boy you want to get to know, talking more and emphasising the accomplishments in your life that have made you feel good about yourself can be helpful.

So, what's important to teenage boys? Let's take a look at what one average 16-year-old boy, Julian, had to say when he was asked

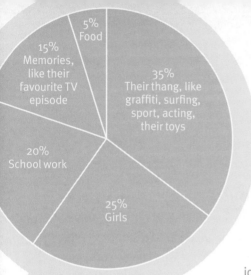

5%
Food

15%
Memories,
like their
favourite TV
episode

35%
Their thang, like
graffiti, surfing,
sport, acting,
their toys

20%
School work

25%
Girls

that question. While it's not the absolute of what all 16-year-old boys are talking about, it's a start to give us an idea that they are actually not just thinking about girls 24/7. Phew!

Research into the difference between boys' and girls' conversation styles by Kathleen Michael showed that boys' talk is mostly about the things they do, like surfing, playing ball, doing art like graffiti, internet games, music, and YouTube events they tend to play over and over to get a laugh. Their opinions about social events occurring in their local and bigger worldwide web is the stuff they get into. Not forgetting, of course, boys' passion for their toys—their PCs, their phones, their electronic toys, their bikes, their cars, the list goes on and on.

Whereas girls, as we all know, spend a lot of time talking about the complex world of our friends and how we feel about what she said, about what you thought about her and what you might think she may think about you. Then there are the complexities of what each of us is going to wear to that party on Friday night or what we can borrow to wear to that party. Now that's not saying we girls don't talk about important things like school assignments, workloads, our part-time jobs or what our parents have said to us this week. It's just where the majority of our time is spent when we are talking with our friends.

It's true that girls are more complex at a younger age in the way they talk to each other, including lots of detail, colour and moment-by-moment accounts in their conversations. And when the boys are not there in the girls' talking circle or lunchtime conversation, it is very different to when they are present in the group. It seems that boys keep the same conversation going whether the girls are there or not! But when the boys and girls come out to play and join together in the group, the talking will seem to follow the lead of the boys' talk more.

'The expression "That's so gay" to describe something stupid wouldn't be seen as rude by a lot of girls and boys, but saying something like "She is a slut" to describe a girl that they know has had sex already can be really sexist and can cause a lot of damage.'—*Domino, age 19*

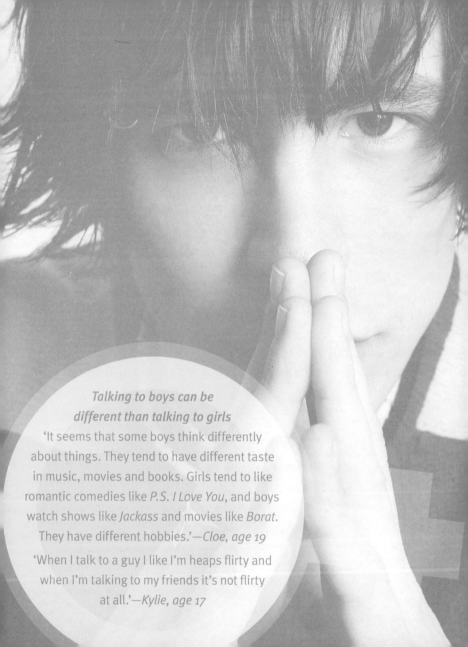

***Talking to boys can be
different than talking to girls***

'It seems that some boys think differently
about things. They tend to have different taste
in music, movies and books. Girls tend to like
romantic comedies like *P.S. I Love You*, and boys
watch shows like *Jackass* and movies like *Borat*.
They have different hobbies.'—*Cloe, age 19*

'When I talk to a guy I like I'm heaps flirty and
when I'm talking to my friends it's not flirty
at all.'—*Kylie, age 17*

Lost in translation

Boys sometimes need a translator when it comes to trying to actually understand what the 'hell' we girls are trying to say. Boys just don't know how to take us girls, especially when we talk backwards, upside down and inside out. Don't worry, boys have their own coded ways of talking too, the most obvious one being using jokes to start getting close to you and to share their personality with you.

Backwards talk (sarcasm)

The girl who says the exact opposite of what she really wants is a backwards talker.

Sarcasm is saying one thing while meaning the complete opposite. For example, when 'sick bitch' is used to describe a girl who is not actually sick, but rather thinks she has all the answers.

The girl who says the exact opposite of what she really wants is a backwards talker. Boys can take sarcasm completely the wrong way, so perhaps when you get to the really important parts of the conversation with that boy who wants to get to know you, be clear (say what you mean) and don't talk backwards.

Upside down talk (bitchiness)

To 'bitch' is to be nasty about somebody or to complain continually. Bitchiness can draw a long arrow back to some low self-esteem or simply can come out to play when you are feeling hungry, angry, lonely, tired or way too serious. It's hard to imagine beautiful girls becoming so ferocious, but it's true. If you are feeling great about yourself there isn't really any need to put anyone upside down with your tongue or to complain, but the truth is there can be a little bit of the bitch in all of us! (Not that anyone likes to admit this, including me.)

I find that using the 'HALTS' is a good way to help me ensure I am not letting the tiger in me out of the cage:

- **HUNGRY?** Make sure I eat regular meals.

- **ANGRY?** Who can I talk to, to get rid of my anger?

- **LONELY?** Why can't I call a friend?

- **TIRED?** Am I getting enough sleep in between my busy life?

- **SERIOUS?** Learn to have more fun and laugh.

> Not talking can be just as deadly
> and in some ways even worse.

If you find yourself in the firing line of girls being bitchy towards you, then you might need to draw a line in the sand. 'Stop, calling me a slut. I was only talking to that boy.'

Teenage girls can become quite predatory over that boy they want to talk to, and if you look like a threat (just because you are capable of being confident) the nails could definitely come out. It is no girl's right to be mean to another girl for just talking to a boy, even if you did have your eye on him first, but the reality is, it happens!

The other form of 'bitching' is the silent treatment—being excluded or being shut down. Not talking can be just as deadly and in some ways even worse, because it is so subtle in its use among girls.

Inside out (flirting)

Flirting is being playful and using your female sexuality in an inside-out type of fashion that shows you really want to attract a boy's attention. Like walking past a boy (a lot), not just coincidently but intentionally. Being over-friendly can sometimes be interpreted as flirting, too. It's simple: save your flirting for the boy who you are really attracted to, not for all boys in the general population! Some of you may even feel you need some flirting lessons. The trick here is, the more confident you feel in your body, the more you'll love the body you have today—not the one you hope to get by going on some ridiculous diet for the next six months—and the more confident you will be with flirting.

Did he get your talk?

Only you can identify your style of talking! Whether you see yourself as the 'deep and meaningful talker', the 'airhead', the 'swearing like one of the boys' type or the 'girl that can just be herself', be aware of those times when your 'talk' may come out backwards, upside down or inside out, and totally confuse any sensible conversation that boy might have been trying to have with you. Maybe we don't even realise that the way we talk and the way we come across to boys may be the very thing that keeps them away from us! Just because the way we talk to family and close friends works, it doesn't mean it's automatically going to work when we talk to that boy. Simply ask him, if the conversation starts to go all weird, 'Did you understand what I was trying to

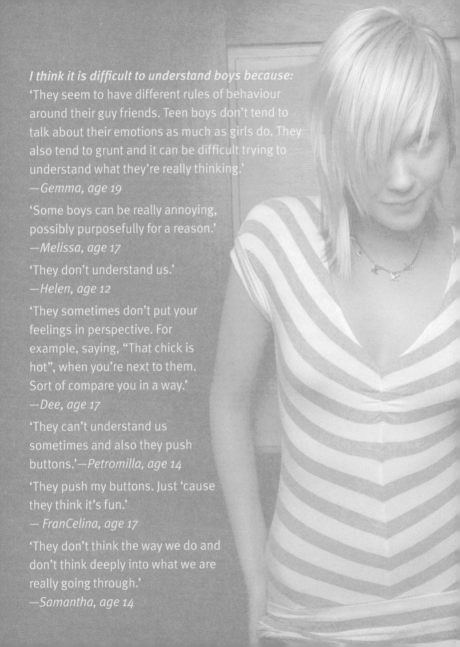

I think it is difficult to understand boys because:

'They seem to have different rules of behaviour around their guy friends. Teen boys don't tend to talk about their emotions as much as girls do. They also tend to grunt and it can be difficult trying to understand what they're really thinking.'
—*Gemma, age 19*

'Some boys can be really annoying, possibly purposefully for a reason.'
—*Melissa, age 17*

'They don't understand us.'
—*Helen, age 12*

'They sometimes don't put your feelings in perspective. For example, saying, "That chick is hot", when you're next to them. Sort of compare you in a way.'
—*Dee, age 17*

'They can't understand us sometimes and also they push buttons.'—*Petromilla, age 14*

'They push my buttons. Just 'cause they think it's fun.'
— *FranCelina, age 17*

'They don't think the way we do and don't think deeply into what we are really going through.'
—*Samantha, age 14*

say?' And let him say back to you what it was you were saying, and then you will really know if he was listening.

Boys and their feelings

If we go back to prehistoric times, the man went out hunting to find and fix the problem. Today, if a boy wants to talk about his feelings or seek help to work out girls, who does he talk to? Where does he go when it comes to working out his stuff, his feelings and concerns?.

According to a 2002 Kids Help Line survey, younger boys (5–9) are the most comfortable talking about their feelings and concerns, and older boys (15–18) are also willing to talk about their feelings. It's the boys in the middle (10–14) who are most uncomfortable talking about how they feel.

According to the same survey, it seems that boys would like to talk more often about their feelings, but there are certain things that stop them:

- Concern about being judged as stupid, crazy, uncool or strange.
- Fear that they will be seen as just 'whinging'.
- The assumption, based on past experiences, that if they do share their feelings they will be ignored or rejected.
- That it would be seen as a sign of weakness to share feelings.
- Concern that if peers found out they had shared their feelings they would be teased and laughed at.
- The worry that once they share their feelings they might not be able to control their emotions.

'Most males bottle up their feelings and then that can be dangerous—it may harm themselves—not good to keep things in.'—*Boy, age 16*

(Source: KHL Newsletter, April 2003.)

Girls, a simple question like: 'How are you feeling right now?' might just be the key to open up that boy to talk about something he may need to get off his chest.

Who to talk to about talking to boys

Only one out of 25 girls aged around 15 years who I interviewed felt comfortable to admit that she didn't know how to talk to boys. Did that mean the other 24 girls were confident in all areas of talking to boys? No. It was clarified in our discussions that while the majority of them felt comfortable simply talking to boys as friends, that when the dynamics changed and there were feelings of excitement, curiosity, intrigue and happiness, and the 'gushiness'—that whirly-girly feeling—started to increase towards a particular boy, the talking moved to the a new level of difficulty. Some were finding this easier than others. There were degrees of stress, not feeling equipped, not knowing where to go with the conversation, and not knowing who to talk to either about the next stage of boy + girl friendship that would potentially move towards the boy + friend equalling boyfriend. It's a whole new level of sexual attraction to negotiate and comprehend.

With this same group of girls there was also a strong consensus that talking to boys wasn't a subject they felt they could go to their adult world for advice about. The ones who did feel they had an adult they could talk to chose big sisters and their mothers, and there was one girl who said there was 'a newly married couple that she felt were really cool and in love' to whom she could talk to about anything because they were closer to her age. I was left wondering whether most teenage girls felt the same—that their adult world wasn't approachable for the conversations they needed to have about boys. While it's great to talk to friends about these 'brave new frontier' topics, it helps to have a more experienced person to make sure you keep your relationships with boys safe and fun. Failing that, educators and books like this one can give you all the information you need at your fingertips.

'Even though we may all be able to talk to boys, it doesn't necessarily mean we are communicating on the same page as boys. It's getting on the same page that can be the tricky bit, especially when the boy we are talking to becomes more than a friend.'—*Keisha, age 15*

3

So, you
want to talk
to boys....

Girls, consider that at every age the reasons you will have for wanting to talk to boys will change. At 12 you may not want to know boys at all, and probably with good reason, as they develop differently and can appear a whole lot younger than us at this age. But as soon as we move into our teens, and our bodies and minds start to even out, our reasons for wanting to talk to boys are suddenly very different. When you are in your early teens, boys can seem like a bit of fun and cool to hang out with, but once we start to feel those natural, normal tingling sensations inside our body (especially around our sensitive reproductive areas), not just inside our thinking, that tell us 'he's cute', it can change entirely the way we talk to boys. This is really important to be conscious of, girls, because you will not feel this way towards all boys—don't worry, that special feeling will only happen for someone to whom you have a natural, healthy attraction.

Just looking ... then something happens

Why is it that one moment we girls are just seeing boys as nice, and good to talk to, and then something changes—we start to have feelings and notice a sense of attraction to that one boy in

I have my own reasons
why I want to talk to boys?
'It's fun.'—*Tia, age 13*
'Boys are easier to talk to than
girls since girls can be extremely
bitchy and gossip heaps.'
—*Peta, age 17*

particular? Our reasons, our motivation to talk to boys changes as we change and develop from girls into young women.

The hormones running through our bodies start to make the necessary natural changes that are programming us to be interested in boys to talk to and get to know. That sounds like we are back in the jungle, but as you change first from a young girl to a young teen, then to a young lady, the 'gut feelings' and natural urges you have to want to be with a special boy will become stronger.

When you start to understand how attraction works, to know how boys think and the special things that trigger those tingling feelings of sexual attraction, you will feel a lot more confident in talking to boys, and you'll be able to start to recognise the ways in which you might change, too, when those boys are around.

Ages and stages
10–12 years

In your pre- to early teens, talking to boys starts out as fun and easy. Boys are still considered 'just friends', and while at first girls move slightly ahead on the physical development front, boys will catch up at around the 16-years-of-age mark.

12–16 years

There can almost be an itchy and scratchy new way of talking among girls at this age. Some may call this bitchiness or mood swings. Hormones are rising, bodies are blooming and puberty is ripe among girls. There can be many frustrations felt in adapting to the natural stages of life development, and what's fair and what's not about just being a girl. Your sexual attraction to boys is waking up and your head space is really just adapting to getting to know your own changing body. Your first period, or 'menarche', arrives, which is the first physical sign that your body has matured and is now ready to start releasing an egg in your monthly menstrual cycle. Your body is now entering its reproduction-readiness phase. That's big, and, yes, full of responsibility, which will require plenty of emotional readiness and mature thinking. While your friends, peer groups and boys are very important to you right now, it is absolutely essential that you don't lose your own individual voice about what is right for you during this tumultuous time of physical change.

16–18 years

Most girls have fully developed into young women, and 'flirting' with your new-found 'girlyness' or 'womanhood' can almost feel natural if there are boys about. That is, you will be consciously aware of your body's attractiveness to boys. Generally, both physically and emotionally, girls talking to boys is a lot more practised by this age.

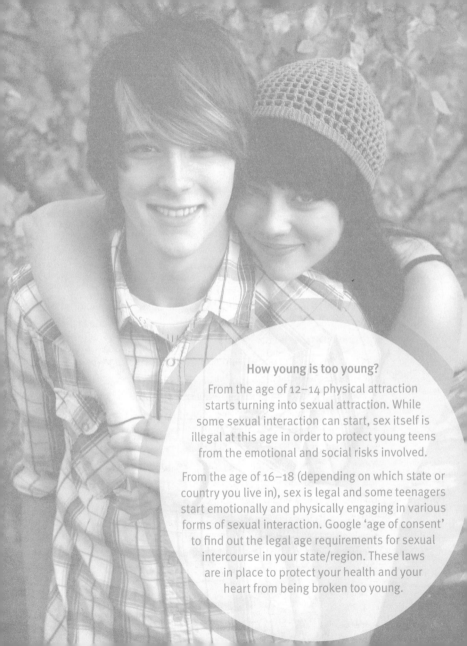

How young is too young?

From the age of 12–14 physical attraction starts turning into sexual attraction. While some sexual interaction can start, sex itself is illegal at this age in order to protect young teens from the emotional and social risks involved.

From the age of 16–18 (depending on which state or country you live in), sex is legal and some teenagers start emotionally and physically engaging in various forms of sexual interaction. Google 'age of consent' to find out the legal age requirements for sexual intercourse in your state/region. These laws are in place to protect your health and your heart from being broken too young.

Pass it on ...

An 18-year-old girl sent me the following email she received in her school email account. I found these facts not alarming but confirming of what I understand is the reality of girls talking to boys and becoming overwhelmed by the natural sexual urges that happen with the onset of hormones kicking in during our teen years.

Subject: FW: It's For Your Safety ...
From: **FRIEND @ SCHOOL**
Date: 19 April 2010 11:37:42 AM

Have you noticed the increasing number of adolescent people interacting in sexual activity? Facts may make youths less likely to engage in sexual activity and increase sexual health.

- Laws that result in our decision could include: Eg. Legal age to have sex is 16 in New South Wales.
- Family and culture can influence our decision and actions on our sexual health. Eg. No sex before marriage.
- Most young people in Years 10 and 12 are sexually active to varying degrees. Selected statistics include: About one in four Year 10 students and half of all Year 12 students have had sexual intercourse. Of the young people who had ever had sex, about half of the males and 61 per cent of the females had at least one sexual partner in the last year.
- Peer Groups and friends can have an impact.
- We are influenced by the action of others in our peer groups.
- Peer pressure to do the same as everyone around us.

A piece of advice from one of my peers to young girls

Talking to boys will most likely be pushing its way to being your highest priority, perhaps even more important than your friendships with your girlfriends, your schoolwork, your favourite TV show or your sport. Some conversations and experiences may leave you feeling as though you wish the earth would open up and swallow you. There is a beautiful innocence in these moments of learning that can often be lost to pride or embarrassment, so remember your experience of learning relationships with boys with delight and kindness to yourself.

– Jacqueline Jayne (age 34)

Older boys and boys who are not ready

There are a lot of things that may get in the way of getting to know that boy you want so much to talk to. He may be more interested in his sport, or still getting over that last girl who broke his heart. You may have noticed him, but he isn't ready for serious talking to girls yet.

It's important to note that boys tend to mature later than girls, and that may be the very reason girls sometimes find that talking to boys their own age can be like talking to a friend whereas talking to older boys can get your heart pumping.

If you are attracted to older guys, let's say you are 16 and he is 22—that's six years' difference—it can be a whole other ball game when you are this young (although not so much when you are in your late twenties and older). The age difference is more difficult when you are still young because, sexually, he will have much more mature thinking and expectations.

Two to three years' older is pretty normal when you are 16, but too much more of a gap can take you to a whole new level—you really need to get clear about what you are entering into with this 'young man', because he is really no longer a boy!

4

First
impressions

Love at first glance

Girls love shopping, and when a girl glances into a shop window and sees that to-die-for, must-have dress, it's almost inevitable that her next words will be, 'I WANT THAT DRESS'. Her eyes take in the colour, the style, the price tag, and then a quick snap decision to purchase it places the dress into the shopping bag. Online shopping has made buying that essential piece for our wardrobe even more immediate: we can sit at the computer with a friend and tell ourselves without even trying it on that it's definitely going to fit. Your mind, your gut feeling, your intuition, the voice inside all let you know at that very first glance that you want it. It's a little bit like talking to boys. We see them either face to face or online, and at first glance something inside of us, our inside world, says, 'I WANT TO TALK TO HIM'.

Shopping and talking to boys? Could there actually be some kind of connection? Yes, it's your intuition at a basic, unconscious level, your very own natural way of summing up if something is pleasant at first glance. But don't be fooled too easily by all that glitters, girls, because 'ALL IS NOT ALWAYS AS IT SEEMS'. Remember that dress you just had to have, no matter what, regardless of the extravagance? You only ever wore it once and it was a complete let down, unlike that other dress that you hang up and make all that extra special effort to keep pretty, the one that never lets you down and is faithful to you every time you put it on.

But if we shopped for boys like we do dresses, what is it that a girl would be looking for at first glance?

- Eyes that can meet her gaze.
- A boy that stands tall and confident in the crowd; definitely no slumping.
- No fidgeting—a dead giveaway for nerves.
- A leader, not the follow-the-leader type.
- A boy who gets his self-esteem from doing the things he loves.

A cute boy

Thinking that a boy is cute is a really good start to wanting to talk to that boy, and also a very natural reason to. He might even be wearing your favourite shade of blue, and this gives you a spark of attraction. However, finding out who the boy is inside the hot t-shirt is actually much more important. Attraction is important but it's only half of the picture; the next essential ingredient you will need if you want to keep talking to this boy for a while is 'time' to get to know him.

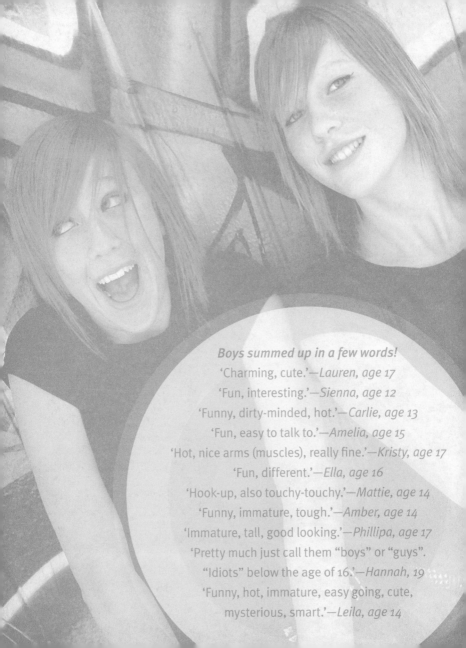

Boys summed up in a few words!

'Charming, cute.'—*Lauren, age 17*

'Fun, interesting.'—*Sienna, age 12*

'Funny, dirty-minded, hot.'—*Carlie, age 13*

'Fun, easy to talk to.'—*Amelia, age 15*

'Hot, nice arms (muscles), really fine.'—*Kristy, age 17*

'Fun, different.'—*Ella, age 16*

'Hook-up, also touchy-touchy.'—*Mattie, age 14*

'Funny, immature, tough.'—*Amber, age 14*

'Immature, tall, good looking.'—*Phillipa, age 17*

'Pretty much just call them "boys" or "guys".
"Idiots" below the age of 16.'—*Hannah, 19*

'Funny, hot, immature, easy going, cute,
mysterious, smart.'—*Leila, age 14*

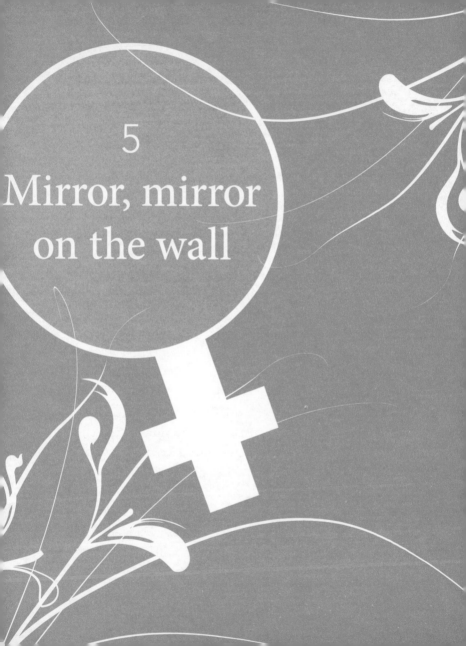

5

Mirror, mirror on the wall

Does the mirror lie to us, or do our girlfriends tell us we look good when we actually don't? Actually, you are the best one to answer this question, and often this can be determined by your feelings and whether you are feeling good about yourself or not.

When we walk out the front door to talk to boys, be aware that the way we put our look together, our total package—our clothes, hair, makeup or no makeup—is an outward reflection of our internal world.

I would like to tell you people don't judge us by how we look. But in the real world, do you see unattractive people presenting the news or on celebrity host shows? No. We see pleasing-to-look-at people who are appropriately dressed for the situation. (If a news presenter wore a really low-cut top with boobies showing off to the world, I can't imagine how much of the news would be heard. OMG!) That's not to say that first impressions are everything, or even the most important thing, but they do count, so it's important you send the right message out when you're putting your look together.

Boobies and booties ...

So what are boys thinking when it comes to girls? Boobies! Boobies! And more boobies! In the same way it is for girls during their teen years, boys' hormones control a lot of what is driving their thoughts. Huge physical changes as well as emotional changes are happening for all of you, and sexual attraction is big for both boys and girls. We are all programmed naturally to admire the female body and the male body. Some girls like big muscles and a six pack, while others might just love red hair and freckles. Yes, girls, it's true—just as we like looking at them, they like looking at us, too. And some of us are too shy to admit this might even be happening right now!

Girls, the way to get to know what anyone is thinking is to ask them, especially boys! The essential key here is do you really want to know what this boy is thinking or do you just like the way he looks?

How to Talk to Girls tells us that boys spend a lot of time just thinking about ... BOOBIES when they think about talking to girls. OMG, girls, if this is really true, then why are we spending

> 'Cleavage can be done in a tasteful manner—
> you can be intelligent, sexy, and not have boobs
> everywhere.'— *Carrie Underwood, multi-platinum-*
> *selling country singer and former* American Idol *winner*

so much time in front of the mirror doing hair and makeup? And then what if, in fact, you don't have boobies? Is there any hope of really finding a boy and talking to him if we know this is what they are programmed biologically to think? Yes, of course! There are boys who know that their penis will erect as soon as they see a beautiful girl; this is natural and healthy, and he will have been having uncontrollable erections since he started puberty and would be very used to dealing with this. Girls, don't worry, you won't even notice this if you are out and about, a bit like a boy never really knows you have a period unless you say something.

The female body is really a beautiful picture; there are many beautiful images of naked women in every famous gallery in the world. It's just that the other extreme—pornography and the sexualisation of girls in glossy magazines—gives an impression that our bodies are just a pleasure centre for anyone to grab at any time! Not the case! Your body is your temple. It's the only one you have to carry you through your entire life, so any damage you make to it, anything you allow it to get involved with, will stay with you forever.

First impressions

Sure, wear a bikini at the beach, but wearing the skimpy nothing outfit that shows all will also say something about you to others. So love your sexuality, love being a girl and love your body, but let boys know you respect you first! If you are not sure how to put your look together, what clothes work with what and how you can look your best, ask for help: Google 'fashion tips'.

For some girls it is difficult to get the right balance between showing themselves off to the world versus showing too much. There is something attractive about showing off a wholesome you rather than dressing to what you think boys want to see.

Every picture tells a thousand words, so I asked some girls between the ages of 12 and 17 to tell me what they thought about the girls in these pictures. I just want you to know that what you wear, how you dress, tells a story to boys (and other girls!), and definitely doesn't give a complete picture of the girl you are today or the woman you want to be one day. Be careful and mindful of the way you come across by the choices you make about what you wear. And be incredibly sensible about the images you choose to place up on any internet site, as unfortunately you will be critiqued!

The following comments on the images of girls and the way they are dressed gives you an example of how easy it is for others to form an opinion about us before they even bother to get to know the real you. Remember that boys will also be taking in the way you look as a message about how to connect with you.

Girl, age 17 @ the end of the night after drinking.

Girls at a fancy-dress 'playboy bunny' party, age 17 and 18.

Girls at an eighteenth birthday party.

Girl shopping, age 18.

Girls out nightclubbing, age 18 and 17.

Girls' responses to image 1:
1. 'Trashy/stupid.' 2. 'OMG.'
3. 'Skinny, slut.' 4. 'Slut.' 5. 'Trashy/
unfriendly/easy (sexual) bogan.'
6. 'Uh, not that hard to get.'
7. 'Hussy. Easy to get, slutty.'
8. 'Not hard to get, slutty, bogan.'

Girls' responses to image 2:
1. 'Cheap/hot.' 2. 'Cheap and slutty.'
3. 'Cheap, I only want her for sex.'
4. 'Scary.' 5. 'Skanky/cheap/only
good for sex.' 6. 'Hot, sexy, easy to
get.' 7. 'Cheap, skanky, easy to get
some.' 8. 'Cheap/skanky.'

Girls' responses to image 3:
1. 'Innocent/cute.' 2. 'I dunno.'
3. 'Hard to get, walk right past her.'
4. 'Pretty.' 5. 'Friendly/natural/friend
vibes.' 6. 'Pretty, fun, hard to get.'
7. 'Unnoticeable.' 8. 'Not noticeable.'

Girls' responses to image 4.
1. 'Pretty.' 2. 'Pretty hot.' 3. 'Pretty.'
4. 'Hot.' 5. 'Hot/pretty/easy to
approach.' 6. 'Nice, decent, hard
to get.' 7. 'Pretty, hard to get.'
8. 'Pretty.'

Girls' responses to image 5.
1. 'Hot/suitable/appropriate.'
2. 'Alright.' 3. 'Pretty.' 4. 'Hotties.'
5. 'Decent/easy to approach.'
6. 'Pretty, kind and shy.' 7. 'Decent,
boy will look.' 8. 'Decent.'

Many girls seem to neglect the fact that the decisions they make about how they dress will influence the way others see them. If you wear practically nothing to a playboy bunny party, it's really an open invitation to boys to check you out, and it may even change friends' opinions about you. Sure, go dressed up, but do it with style, without showing off your entire body. Find a middle way to be yourself and have fun without jeopardising your reputation.

Comparing our outsides to our insides

Girls, are we all getting too critical of ourselves, I mean in the way we 'talk to ourselves'? That is, in the words we tell ourselves in the secrecy of our own mind, or in the mirror—the classic ones being, 'I'm too fat, I'm too short', and 'My hair is too thin, too thick', or 'I don't look as good as she looks'.

Are we comparing our outsides to our insides? Are we comparing the way we talk to the way we see some older girls talk, or our older sister, or the way we see our favourite rock star or famous artist talk in interviews, and are we trying to shape the way we talk based on them? Do you have enough confidence in yourself and the way you talk about your thang to boys? Consider that the way you see yourself can, in some ways, be projected out to others. For example, you may lack confidence in your own abilities and be the type of girl who continually has to ask others what they think about you. 'Does this dress look good on me?' Asking this over and over to your friends can become painful not just for you, but for your friends, too!

Learning to trust what you think about you is the key! You just need to find a level of confidence in your decisions about the way you will talk to boys. Just like working out which style of jeans works really well on your body, a lot of your style in talking to boys will only come with practice. You might be a girl who doesn't have even one pair of jeans you like and only wears skirts and dresses. As long as you find a natural flow of more positive than negative thinking, I can safely say that in time you will start attracting boys, just because you have a good sense of who you are. Most boys like that.

The reality is, people in general do judge books by their covers. The good news is that the way you look, the way you present yourself to boys, is entirely up to you. You make the choices every time you get dressed ready to go out into that big wide world.

A 2006 Girl Scouts USA study found that, for most girls, being healthy has more to do with appearing 'normal' and feeling accepted than maintaining good diet and exercise habits. On the one hand girls are told to be happy with the way they are, and on the other they are given the message that being 'overweight' is unhealthy and unattractive.

The same study found that a mother's weight, body image, attitude and healthy habits are strong indicators of whether her daughter is overweight, satisfied with her body and physically active. Girls look to their mothers for advice on healthy living. A daughter's dissatisfaction with her weight is greater if her mother is also dissatisfied with her own weight, despite how much a daughter actually weighs.

6
Believe
in you

Naturally confident?

Sorry, girls, you can't buy this one in a shop; it has to be earnt and learnt, and made to specially fit you. Actually, confidence is the single most attractive thing any girl can have right at her fingertips. But be warned, you can't fake it, but you can work on building your own confidence right here, right now. Your confidence is your glow. It's your reputation, the part of you that stands out when you have left the party, that special factor that gets that boy wanting to know you and, most likely, wanting to track down your number.

• Why are you the girl that boy wants to talk to?

Write down the things you think are great about you? Are you faithful? Are you genuine? Make sure you know what you like about you, otherwise it will be pretty hard to convince that boy if you're not even sure yourself. And just for the record, despite the judgements we all make based on appearances, at the end of the day it's the girl inside the outfit that is special, not the outfit that you have probably spent hours preparing. Be relaxed, be the real you!

The boys or girls who judge you by what you wear don't matter. The girls and boys that matter won't actually mind what you wear. They are more interested in you!

• Fun is the most important goal

If you have fun so will he, and the easier it will be to get to know each other. You're not meant to test him, like a quiz he needs to pass. Just chill and make sure you get him talking about himself.

• Let him be the 'boy' and you be the 'girl'

If he wants to be the leader on the 'getting to know you' time, let him show you who he is. There will be plenty of time for you to let him know all the things you like. Even though girls are great leaders too, during this girl–boy 'getting to know you' dance it will be wise in the first instance, girls, to let him show you his lead in talking to you.

• Dress to impress

When you look into the mirror, are you happy with the way you present yourself to all those boys out there as soon as you leave your front door?

Being naturally confident by feeling attractive, loving the body you have got and the looks you have been given, and learning how to dress to impress for all situations can come easier for some of us than for others, no matter how hard we try. Get help if you can to improve your image if you are not happy—it's okay to do this. Unfortunately we really do get judged on our appearances. I'd like to tell you this doesn't happen, but that would be unfair. But everyone can, with help, look fantabulous! I am certain of this.

My understanding of the good looks department is that there will always be someone better looking than you in this world and, likewise, there will always be someone who is not as good looking as you. That makes everything feel a whole lot fairer to me. Especially when you want to trust the boy you are starting to get to know, there is no room to start getting jealous of every other girl he talks to; this will not help at all!

Staying on track with your own plans

Girls who inspire and have their own personal vision are leaders. They make plans. They keep making the necessary changes until this vision is reached. They lead by example, and then others want to come into their vision.

Respect and trust are a given with your friends; you want others to know the way you trust and respect them is what you deserve, too, especially when you are not around.

So how do you remain focused and achieve your own goals, especially when boys can be such a big distraction? Ensure you have a clear focus on a goal and devote specific time to this goal, and then you will naturally find you start to hang out with girls who have the same goals.

What are some of the stumbling blocks you may come across in working towards a healthier self-confidence? Perhaps you may relate to some old patterns that keep stopping you from being your best. OMG, this can be hard to stay on track! But once you start to feel good about yourself, it's all worth it.

Physical wellbeing

Back to how we look. The way you present yourself is a telltale message to the world. Rightly or wrongly, this view of you, your posture and your body language gives everyone a ready image of how you value yourself. If you are really overweight this may say one of a number of things, like 'I don't care about my physical wellbeing', or 'I have a medical condition, like an eating disorder'. If, on the other hand, you are extremely thin, it can say exactly the same thing. Somewhere in the healthy middle range that respectfully suits your personality and lifestyle usually works best. And yes, the battle of weight is a huge issue for girls, but it is possible to find a healthy balance of diet, lifestyle and exercise that will work for you. But, girls, it's not going to come and find you. You have to get up off your butt and go and get it!

Improve the way you talk

Communication is getting your ideas across clearly by talking and listening. Earlier I mentioned that the way you talk, the way you communicate, might be the direct result of how you were taught to do so by your family. If this works, great! But if there is some room

According to the Dove Campaign for Real Beauty, 92% of teen girls would like to change something about the way they look, with body weight ranking the highest. 'Not only do women agree that happiness is the primary element making a woman beautiful, but they strongly agree that they themselves feel most beautiful when they are happy and fulfilled in their lives (86%). Women want younger generations of girls and women to inherit this broader concept of beauty, with 82% strongly agreeing that, "If I had a daughter, I would want her to feel beautiful, even if she was not physically attractive".'

—*Dove Campaign for Real Beauty* (Unilever) 'Beyond Stereotypes: Rebuilding the Foundation of Beauty Beliefs' (2006) and 'Real Truth About Beauty' (2005) global studies.

for improvement, ask for help. In my home, when my mum and dad had an argument, everyone stopped talking—it was pretty icy at times. Today, if I am really angry, I can still go back to that habit of ignoring rather than facing up to my side of cleaning up the mess. Changing your habits takes courage and a level of self-honesty. You may learn your own way of talking that helps you to build clear, healthy, two-way channels of communication. Remember, if you are not getting along with your friends most of the time, it may be time to have a look at the way you talk to them!

Know yourself

To thy own self be true! What is your truest self? Who are you really? Do you know your own signature strengths—the things about you that shine and show your self-confidence?

Knowing what you like and dislike, what sparks your interest and what challenges you all helps you in making everyday decisions that move you towards your heart's desires.

Are you leadership material?

Working on your self-confidence, the things that give your self-esteem a glow, you may find yourself as a leader in your group of girlfriends, always being asked by others in the group what you think on everything from where you are going this weekend to what subjects choices you are taking in your final years of school, and even how to deal with parents that just won't let you out.

At times you may even find yourself being asked advice by

other girls or other boys on how to talk to boys or vice versa. Be especially careful to guide but not tell, to present the possible choices rather than make decisions on other people's behalf. A strong leader, a girl with confidence, doesn't need to run everyone else's lives—her own is full enough! Sometimes not having all the answers shows humility and will inspire your girlfriends to learn how to start listening to their own gut feeling.

Influence is built on the trust and loyalty of your friends, so be mindful because at times your influence may be able to change other girls' and boys' opinions. Again, expecting to be treated with respect and trust, but at the other extreme influence can go to some girl's heads, resulting in the misuse of power. Let me be very clear here, leadership is based on others' attraction to who you are—your wholesome self, your inside and outside, the way you respect yourself and others, the way you keep your own dreams in sight. It is not the promotion of being the most popular or having the most friends. So if you are in a popular position in a dominant group of girls and have influence over others that may make you feel important, remember to use your influence responsibly and treat your friends with respect.

7

Respect

Respect for yourself is an essential, non-negotiable ingredient when talking to boys. Let's face it, if we can't respect ourselves then why should we expect the boys we are talking to to respect us? Yet sometimes we treat others better than we are able to treat ourselves. While you may be able to do something with a friend or for a friend, like go on a jog to get fit because your friend wants to get healthy, the motivation to do that for yourself may be a complete struggle. To actually motivate yourself to get off the lounge after school or out of bed early in the morning to do a 20-minute run may seem like climbing Mount Everest. Recognising what you need to do for yourself is the first step up the mountain of self-respect. The first one we have this responsibility to is ourselves.

Confucius says: respect yourself and others will respect you

Knowing how to admire the girl you are, to value the things you believe in like your family and all your strengths, and able to show appreciation for the way you have been brought up in this world are all ways to note how much self-respect you have acquired to date.

Being completely true to yourself is the critical starting point of how best to talk to boys.

Sometimes a lack of self-respect comes under the guise of always putting others' needs ahead of your own, so that at the end of the day you're too busy to do the things you need to keep a healthy body and mind.

Stand tall and feel proud the next time you say no, because you have to look after your own needs before you can look after those of others. This is called self-preservation and may even give you the time to find out what you are good at! With self-respect comes the ability to be honest, open-minded and willing to speak your truth. That's right, not what you think your friends want to hear, but what is right for you. Sounds simple, but actually it's not easy if you come from a place where you just want everyone to like you, including boys. Unfortunately, girls, we cannot buy self-respect from the mall. Respect is priceless as it has to come from within you.

The type of girl who may experience a lot of heartaches and go through a lot of indecision when it comes to talking to boys will most likely be disconnected from her own potential, her own dreams, and definitely will not be clear about her own strengths. Even though she may have a lot going for her on the outside—great

*Do the things that make you feel
love and light and happiness.*

parents, great looks, great clothes, great hair, great friends—this girl might still feel restless, irritable and discontented because she just can't find the connection with herself first.

Knowing and being confident requires building on the things you do for yourself that make you feel good. If going to the gym makes you feel good about your body, go to the gym. If running around the block makes you have more energy, run rabbit, run! If drawing a picture of a flower helps you connect with the things you love, draw till your heart's content. If dancing makes you feel alive and full of spirit, dance your little heart out. If laughing brightens up your world, watch funny films. Do the things that make you feel love and light and happiness, and the whole world (including all the boys on the planet) will see your shine of confidence in the very things that make you feel good about you!

Trust your gut feeling

Of course, you all know your gut feeling. It's that very still, small, quiet voice within you that knows the difference between right and wrong, what's good for you and what's bad for you. It's like an inbuilt tracking system that has your best interest at heart. But learning to trust and listen to your gut feeling can be harder than you might think, especially with the rush of feelings that talking to boys can bring on. So be sure to listen to the whispers of your heart and not fall short of the respect you have for yourself.

The values you have around your body, heart and soul will need to be rock solid, as they will get tested around boys!

Trust me, you will know what to do in any situation when it comes to boys as long as you really learn to listen to your own gut feeling. Some of you may only know your gut feeling as nerves or a tingly feeling in your tummy. In Chapter 14 Connecting with 'me', I go into a bit more detail about how to get still and listen to the quiet voice within; you never know when you are going to need it. And there will come a point, when no girlfriends are around to offer their advice, when it will be entirely up to you to face that boy who has the potential of becoming more than a friend and make your own decisions.

'That party—yes, I really want to go, but I am just not sure about catching trains and I know my parents don't really want me to do that. So no, I can't go. But I am happy to meet you after school with some friends.' Afraid of having your voice? Don't be ridiculous. Saying no to that boy about the party because you value what your parents have taught you is something he will probably just respect you all the more for. Being confident and knowing what you really want is priceless.

No matter what, stick to your gut feeling. Your gut is connected to your heart, and your inside and outside world of happiness

Gut feeling
intuition
spirituality
happiness
tingles
nerves
butterflys

depends on this relationship with yourself. Every girl deserves an abundance of happiness in life, and a connection with a boy that wants this too.

So, what do you believe about you?

Every morning, when you wake up, what is the first thing you say to yourself? That's before you pick up your mobile phone, before you brush your teeth and, especially, before you put on your makeup.

Before you step out of bed and rush into the day, take one special moment to keep yourself on track to be true to you. Try repeating this: 'I am a confident young girl, who has an abundance of self-respect. I can talk to boys with ease, by just being myself.'

Now, if saying this makes you feel like puking, you probably don't believe this to be true for you. The harder the affirmation (positive self-talk) is to say to ourselves the closer we are to saying exactly what we need to hear, so that we can be ourselves, not some cover of a magazine 'trying hard' to be something we are not. When the affirmation you choose for yourself becomes easy to say, then you can usually let it go.

To come up with an affirmation that's right for you, look at any area in your life that you want to improve and set the action you want to achieve. 'I am a strong and confident swimmer. I am able to respect my body by exercising three times per week.' Google 'affirmations' for plenty more ideas.

Remember, boys are not puppy dogs or handbags or prize possessions. Just like you they are human beings first, and the boy worth getting to know wants to know u r in 2 him 2.

Respect for others

When I studied to become a teacher, I was introduced to some great ideas on how we develop and change by two legends in psychology named Jean Piaget and Erik Erikson. They made a big impression on my thinking. They helped me to respect each of us as a 'whole' person. Their ideas made me awake to the idea that when we talk to boys, it's not just the words we speak but the entire way we put our whole self across from the moment we say, 'Hello, what's your name?' If you know you like him and want to see him more, let him know sooner rather than later. While talking to boys may be new, it's not a game, because we are dealing with another human being's emotions. And no one wants to feel rejected or hurt.

Building up a conversation with a boy the first few times will require respect and trust in taking that emotional risk, and a bit of trial and error. Getting to know how he thinks, how he feels and whether he is the type of boy you can feel totally comfortable around will simply take time. So make it fun!

8

In 2 me u c

A window in 2 me!

Tipping a girl's hand bag or school bag upside down and inside out will often give some idea of the things that are important to her, whereas boys generally travel lightly—a wallet in their back pocket and they're out for the day—and are, some would say, a whole lot less complicated.

There are a lot of little windows that reveal things about you to that boy you're talking to who wants to get to know you. Are you really ready for him to c in 2 u? Would you be prepared to tip your bag upside down and let him c u, or is that getting way too personal?

'In 2 me u c' thinking

Will this boy get you? Can he understand who you are? Is he really interested in the things you like, what you stand for, and what you don't like? It's up to you how much information about yourself you decide to give him; after all, what you reveal will help this boy to 'get' the girl you are today, the girl you have been in the past and the girl you want to be. How he connects with you and gets to know you will give you a gut feeling whether or not this boy will stay your friend or become your boyfriend. Intimacy, or 'in 2 me u c', is something you want with someone who really cares and respects you—all of you!

'In 2 me u c' thinking explained!

In = intuition
2   = it takes 2 to talk
Me = simply just being me
U   = you
C   = communication

Your gut feeling about that boy who is fast approaching and wants to talk to you will not let you down in knowing whether he is right for you. You may have given him a signal like a smile to let him know it's okay to approach you, or he may have asked a mutual friend to see if you were open to talking to him, or he may have actually had the confidence to ask you to hang with him. If he really likes you he will definitely start beating a track down to your door. The texts, the messages, the power of 'I WANT TO TALK TO HER' is massive, but, girls, let him do this in his own time. Trust that if he has rung once, he will call again as long as you have encouraged him to do so. Remember, be clear. The last thing he will want is rejection, but if you know in your heart that it's not going to happen even before it starts, be gentle with your no.

'2' = it takes 2 to talk

Whether you are talking face to face or getting to know each other on the internet, it takes two to talk. Talking online rather than face to face may be more risky, but also be aware that there's more opportunity for him to misinterpret what you say. Like 'c u round', to him, might mean that he is just another friend and you'll see him around whenever, rather than 'I want to see you really soon'. So be sure your meaning is clear.

When you talk face to face, you get a brighter, fuller physical picture of his responses to all your questions, and you really start to get to know him. You'll see in his facial expressions if he is enjoying your company, and don't worry if he is looking at you a lot. Try to look back into his eyes when you talk to him; this way he really knows that you are interested in him too. Remember, not all boys are just after your body, nor are they all immature and strange. Well, let's hope not! If he is lost for words, help him out, especially if you are the more motivated talker! If he is not strong with conversation, I am certain there are other areas he will be strong in that you will find out about through this 'getting to know you' time. Not everyone has every single skill when it comes to getting to know someone new for the first time, especially boys.

'Me' = simply just being me

Don't forget little me! That's the little girl inside the big girl you have become. Remember the things that made you happy as a little girl—playing with your dog, going for rides on your bike,

'He thought, when I texted him back, saying, "c u round", that this meant I wasn't really interested in him. But when we talked about this face to face I explained I did want to see him again. My response, I now understand, was a closed response; it didn't invite him to text again. I needed to be clearer, like "Yeah, it would be good to c u real soon?" This would have let him know I was definitely interested. Lucky we saw each other again, face to face.'
—April May, age 18

getting your hair combed ready for school. All the things that made you become you. All your school photos, your Christmas wish lists, your birthday parties. These are all the things you will have to talk about—the list is endless. There is no one on this earth exactly like you and there will never be another you. Don't be shy to start telling your 'little me' story. Boys love hearing that stuff; it makes them feel warm and fuzzy! And he may start to tell you his 'little boy' story too.

'U' = uncover the little boy inside

Who is the boy you are talking to, anyway, and is he the boy who makes your heart sing or is he simply going to be a really good friend? It's up to you to discover who he is, and this needs to be fun, girls. It's not your turn to be detective boy squad! The main thing is, the more comfortable and at ease he is with you, the more he will let down any barriers naturally and allow you to start to get to know the little boy inside.

It's unrealistic to expect him to be relaxed around you all the time at first, but eventually he will be as you uncover the goods on him. There might be stuff that bugs you about him, too; it will probably come out sooner rather than later. If you start noticing little things that irritate you about him, don't be surprised if he starts to observe little things about you that unsettle him too. Unfortunately, none of us are perfect.

'C' = communication

Never assume that all boys, or all girls, for that matter, are excellent communicators. Every girl will come to the 'how to talk to boys' table with a certain level of skill when it comes to making connections with boys. A few essential tips:

- Say exactly what you mean.
- Ask him if he understands what you said. Give him time to talk.
- Listening takes practice. Let him finish the things he feels he needs to say.
- Disagreement and staying true to what you believe in can be healthy.
- Keep him talking, rather than asking yes or no questions.
- Writing a journal of your ideas about him will help you get clearer about your feelings towards the boy you're talking to.
- If the conversation gets stuck or sticky, ask him how he is feeling right now?.

'In 2 me u c' is not a race

'Girl talking to boy' and 'boy talking to girl' is definitely not a race or easy! Take it gently and enjoy each conversation when you're getting to know a boy that is showing interest in you. Just like a flower opening up to the sun each day in its own natural time, you too will open up to a boy if you feel comfortable and if there is some physical attraction present.

Teenage dating talk

Lucy: Good morning, babe.

Toby: Good morning, princess. How did you sleep?

Lucy: Not too bad, but Shelly woke me up.

Toby: Aw, no good. Do you want me to drive you to school?

Lucy: Yes please. I'll see you soon.

Toby: OK, no worries ... be outside in 10. xxx

Ben: Hello, how's it going?

Anna: Hey, yeah I'm good. How about you?

Ben: I'm good, thank you. What's doing?

Anna: Homework and assignments. And you?

Ben: Ahh, same! I hate school, so over it.

Anna: Oh my God, so am I. It's sooo annoying and it's getting harder!

9

It's just not
your thang

It can be such a natural, wonderful thing to want to talk to boys, to be in touch with being a girl and to be wondering what those boys are thinking about us girls—waiting for a text, a ring-tone sound, a sign or even just a simple old-fashioned, 'Hello, what's your name and what school do you go to?' Some girls are just so easy with boys, simply because they are easy with themselves, they like who they are and naturally start getting to know boys just by being their friends. But what if it's not like that for you, and talking to boys brings up fear, doubt and insecurity? What does that mean?

Fear, doubt and insecurity

Fear, doubt and insecurity when it comes to talking to boys are all emotions that can become very real and immensely overwhelming for some girls for a range of different reasons. Some of these reasons may be founded and some may be unfounded. Founded reasons are a result of experiences that may have happened in your life that limit you in some way from being your total 'girl' wholesome self. Unfortunately, there are girls who have been abused or harmed in some way by men or boys, and this in fact distorts the natural,

Feel the fear and breathe—sometimes
we just have to take those risks.

healthy progression of your sexuality when it comes time to start talking to boys.

Seeking help to uncover this harm is essential to claim back the right to a healthy sense of self that every girl deserves when it comes to talking to boys. Over time, counselling can help repair emotional scars, but the sad reality is that many girls will not talk about these events. To experience fear, have doubt or to feel insecure in your gut when talking to boys in these circumstances, when it is linked to these traumatic events in your earlier life, is simply not fair! Each new boy that is trying to talk to you is not your past; he is in your present and may be the one who is able to respect you and who is trying really hard to be in 2 u.

The other kind of fear is based on unfounded reasons—things we make up in our mind, the 'self-talk' that can actually stop us from speaking to that boy who may potentially be really interested. It might be that you are telling yourself 'There is no way that boy will talk to me. He is too good looking for me'. Your fear is so great that when he walks past you, you turn to mush inside and walk the other way before he even gets the chance to talk to you. Stop right there! Turn back around. There is no factual evidence that this boy will not talk to you, so feel the fear and breathe. Sometimes we just have to take those risks when talking to boys, regardless of how they look!

Self-doubt and insecurities will lessen the more you talk to boys. You will learn to trust yourself and take risks, and you'll come to understand that if the boy does keep walking, that's only because you deserve better.

Alcohol and talking to boys

There are some girls who feel they need alcohol to give them confidence when talking to boys, and vice versa. Is that true or is it just a myth? I think that to some degree it is true, in the sense that both girls and boys start experimenting with drinking and the alcohol can sometimes take away inhibitions (fears, doubts or insecurities) that may get in the way of talking to a boy. What is key here is to know that drinking (at a legal age) in moderation sure can be fun and a relaxer, but that alcohol taken to excess can distort what you say to that boy, and if you go as far as to get drunk it can actually lead to short-term memory loss, leaving you in the vulnerable position of not being able to remember what you said to that boy at all. Not a good look!

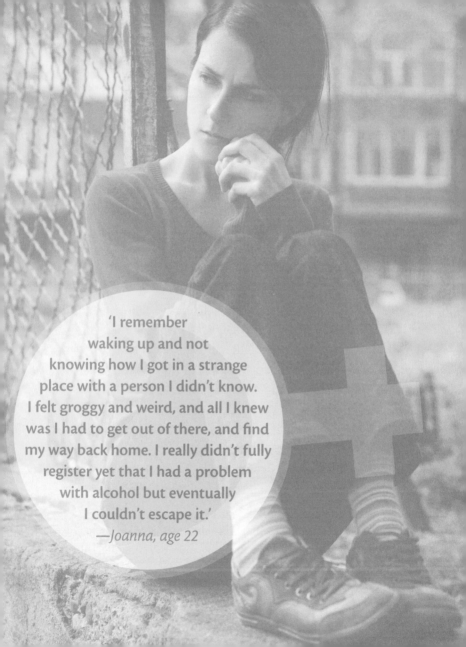

'I remember waking up and not knowing how I got in a strange place with a person I didn't know. I felt groggy and weird, and all I knew was I had to get out of there, and find my way back home. I really didn't fully register yet that I had a problem with alcohol but eventually I couldn't escape it.'
—*Joanna, age 22*

What if I am gay?

Getting comfortable with your sexuality is key for any girl. However, if you are gay—that is, if you are a girl and are sexually attracted to other girls rather than boys—then talking to boys will be a different experience altogether as far as the sexual attraction element goes. It seems the expectation is that all girls will be attracted to boys, which may present challenges if you are gay. However, once you have determined and found confidence with your sexuality, which can be tricky, tiresome and traumatic, the same basic principles of respect and attracting someone to you by doing your thang still apply, regardless of gender. Definitely keep on track with your life and let the natural attraction 'zing' thing happen to you. Waiting for that girl who is in 2 u to find you, just as you would otherwise wait for that boy, is the surest way to get comfortable talking when the chemistry of sexual attraction kicks in.

'My sexuality' *by Kristen Hedgpeth*

[A personal story of a gay girl's experience talking to boys]

I have always had a pretty close relationship with my brothers, and I'd say they are still, to a large extent, my best male friends. We always support each other in our dreams and goals.

Now I relate to most guys like a kind of brother figure, but during my teen and early adult years I related to them more sexually.

I went to mixed public schools as a kid, then to a private girls' high school and then to a fashion college. The boys I talked to at school were often my brothers' friends or my friends' brothers/boyfriends. At college I had a few close (gay) guy friends.

When I was in primary school I remember I loved playing with my boy friends in the sand pit, riding bikes, playing cars and climbing trees. I remember finding catch and kiss scary and creepy!

In early high school, I would talk to boys about homework, games, art, music, films, skateboarding, school, etc. Just general interests and friend stuff. We'd hang out and go to the park, watch TV, etc. Nothing too intimate. When it came to dating we would just add the physically intimate stuff and go from there!

When I was in college, my lovely gay guy friends would accompany me to the coffee shop for long talks about shopping, celebrities, fashion world gossip and moral support around dating. I would talk to them much more intimately than I would a girl friend.

At the age of 12, I remember becoming aware of the expectation to like boys in a romantic way. All the films I'd ever seen and media, in fact everything I'd been exposed to up to that point, pointed to it.

I remember, when I was 13, complaining to my mum how disgusting sex with men seemed, and how I never wanted to get married or have babies or kiss a boy. She just laughed and said, 'One day you'll feel differently'. Funnily enough, I only felt differently when I finally fell in love with a woman, when I was 26.

As a 15 year old, I started to flirt with boys and realised how flattering it felt just to get the attention. I dated a few guys in high school—I felt it was expected. At that point I was still experimenting and wasn't sure if I was gay yet. I'd had some major crushes on girls. The expectation seems to be that most people are straight, so it's a bit of a journey to finding out you're not.

At 17 I started dating girls a bit and really loved it but fought with my own internalised homophobia. Guys seemed safer (in terms of being socially acceptable, especially to my mum)—and easier! I was living [in Sydney] on the north shore and had no exposure to the gay scene, so it seemed easier to flirt with and pick up guys.

By the time I reached 21 I started my first long-term relationship (with a guy), which lasted four years. The whole time I questioned and struggled with my sexuality. He was really my best friend at the time, rather than a lover. We would hang out and have so much fun together playing tricks, travelling and cooking together.

10
Once upon a time ....

Once upon a time not that long ago, boys needed permission to start talking to girls. Good old-fashioned 'courting' was the order of the day. Can you imagine one of your parents needing to be present as chaperone every time you talked to a boy who was interested in you? OMG, imagine if they were expected to intercept every text, every electronic message before you read it. In days gone by, many a letter between a girl and a boy was intercepted by the adults in their world; even I remember getting caught sending a love letter in Year 3. I was all of eight years old—how embarrassing! Thank God Sister Cuthbert just laughed. She has probably long forgotten about that, but I have clearly not!

Today, in every family to varying degrees, there are still rules in place that reflect cultural and religious expectations about the way we have relationships with boys. In some families these rules may be strict, while in others the boundaries are very relaxed. It depends on the family, the country, the culture and the religion you are born into.

Pride and Prejudice

More than two centuries ago, Jane Austen wrote *Pride and Prejudice*, a timeless tale of how girls talk to boys. Her main character, Elizabeth, has intelligence and wit, and knows what she wants, and that includes not abandoning her own dreams, values or beliefs for any boy, even if it is the notable Mr Darcy—the 'hottie', the boy all the girls want. Elizabeth has the self-respect and persistence to stay on her own path, and the determination to be true to herself in spite of her natural compass, her pheromones, the rush, the gushiness, the dizziness that overwhelms her every time Mr Darcy walks into her presence.

Through the dramas that unfold within this world of early 19th-century courting, we see the timeless importance of listening to our gut feelings and getting to know that boy before we rush into falling head over heels in lust and desire for him. At a time in history when girls did not have the same opportunities as boys, the character of Elizabeth found the courage to speak her mind, especially when in the presence of Mr Darcy. She wanted to right the wrongs of injustice, and challenged her right and the rights of others (especially her sisters) to happiness. For the character Mr Darcy, it was not solely his physical attraction to Elizabeth that made him want to 'court' her, it was more his intrigue, his admiration for her love of learning and the way she was comfortable just being herself.

And yes, in the end Mr Darcy comes to Elizabeth like a bee to the centre of a unique, exotic-scented flower without Elizabeth needing to compromise herself in any way, shape or form. It is in this quality of self-respect that we find integrity in the character of Elizabeth and truly believe she has attracted the man (Mr Darcy) that is her destined truest love.

The moral of Jane Austen's story is that if you have respect for yourself, love will follow. The title of her book, *Pride and Prejudice*, describes in a nutshell the two character flaws that can stand between us and the boy who is naturally attracted to us:

Pride = strong sense of one's own value and satisfaction with oneself.

Prejudice = opinions formed beforehand; holding on to an irrational dislike of somebody.

ONCE UPON A TIME . . . .

'According to the "rule book", there are some things that girls and boys shouldn't do around each other, but I personally would probably be comfortable to just be myself around them.'—*Melissa Le, age 17*

I wish I didn't say that!

Girls, you may start talking to boys only to decide you got it all wrong, leaving you wishing you could turn back the clock. Have you ever thought 'If only I didn't say that!'? Keep in mind there is always going to be a next time to keep practising and improving your conversations with boys. In the meantime, here are ten things to avoid:

1. SAVE ALL NEGATIVITY till you get home and open up your diary, or share it with a true girlfriend or someone who is able to hear your real-life complaints. Do you really want to weigh down this new boy with all the bad stuff straight up?

2. SAVE YOUR COMPLETE LIFE STORY. Start getting to know each other and leave him wondering what happens in the next chapter for the next date.

3. EASE UP ON THE SARCASM. If you express what's in your heart by using sarcasm a lot, you may really confuse him. Try to be clear about the serious stuff, like your true feelings for him. Or explain that when you say, 'I hate you', it really means, 'I like you'. You may have to translate your talk.

4. DON'T BE TOO SERIOUS. Throw some fun in there. Laugh and find the little kid inside you—the fun, free-thinking spirit that is very attractive to boys. Your humour might be quirky or come out as sarcasm, but if used in a happy way it can be fun.

5. DON'T ASK HIM OUT. Who asks who out is a big question. It's really the boy's job, girls, to ask us out—remember, he is going to come and find you doing what you love—but there is always the exception to every rule.

   Well then, ask him! It may just work out. He is either going to say yes or no, and you may end up being together happily ever after. If you take the lead in asking him out (and a lot of girls do).

   Be mindful that in the 'girl ask boy out role' you could find yourself down the track wishing he would take the initiative for the stuff you do together.

6. TO KISS OR NOT TO KISS? Do you ask him to kiss you first or will he ask if he can kiss you? Permission to kiss needs to be a mutual and respectful decision made by both of you. Enjoy!

7. YOU WISH YOU COULD TURN BACK THE CLOCK. You may have told his best friend you really like him in the hope he finds out, and then all of a sudden he starts to seek you out. Breathe, and yes, there is a consequence when you put yourself out there. You will get a big rush of feelings as you wait to see what happens next. Keep it light and fun so no one gets hurt until you work out if he is actually the boy you really want to talk to and get to know more.

9. DONT BE SOMEONE YOU ARE NOT. Definitely don't go putting yourself down in front of that boy or changing yourself just to please him. Wrap up your worries and insecurities and put them under your pillow for the worry doll (LOL). You don't need to criticise yourself. No way!

10. LET HIM TALK. Don't be afraid of silence in the conversation. Definitely don't do all the talking; leave enough space for him to let you know who he is.

Advice from girls your own age of what not to do around boys

'Don't burp or discuss bodily functions. Particularly female-specific issues such as periods and tampons. Boys can be very prudish about those sorts of things. It's very easy to talk about those things with other girls but it makes boys feel very uncomfortable. Don't swear too much, it sounds trashy and aggressive. Don't be overly judgemental or criticise other people (your friends, etc.), it makes you look mean/bitchy. Don't think you're top shit, and don't show off. Don't think big of yourself, sick bitch [i.e., a girl who knows everything]. Don't act too clingy and don't be fake. Guys love natural girls. And, again, don't be a sick bitch [a girl who thinks she knows everyone]. Lastly, don't hang around him when he's with his group of friends and show off.'—*High school girls, age 12–17*

11
Getting
connected

It is hard to imagine girls talking to boys today without social networks like My Space, Facebook and mobile phones. Walking out of the house without your mobile phone can leave you feeling disconnected. In a recent study in the United States it was found that 'Nearly all teens, both boys and girls, over the age of 15 will have their own mobiles'. Now, with a quick exchange of a mobile number or email address, we can connect and start exchanging messages before we even have the time to make up our mind if we are going to put the effort that will be required into getting to know that boy. It's so much easier to text and write than it is to talk face to face. Face to face requires being fully present in the moment of the conversation, whereas electronic messaging gives you much more time to think about your response. Sometimes too much time!

Recently, I watched a girl in her late teens walk by a boy on the street. They looked like they knew each other by the way they smiled, but the conversation was brief as she appeared to be too busy to stop and talk. He seemed somewhat disappointed that he couldn't get her full attention, so he called out to her as she was walking away up the street, 'Hey, have you got my mobile number?'

Next thing he is shouting out his number to her down the street at the top of his lungs!

Exchanging a hotmail address or your web details can be as easy as that. You can't talk right now, but you have a number. So what do you say when it comes time to talk?

Text messaging

Once you have exchanged numbers, and it was a mutual exchange—that is, you both wanted to swap numbers, as opposed to someone else passing out your number—who calls first? I have not seen any rule book when it comes to who should call or text first, but a simple 'Hello' will usually get an immediate response if he wants to get to know you. If, on the other hand, you hear nothing for a couple of days or a week, let it go!

If he sends a text saying, 'What's up?', rather than just replying, 'Not much', perhaps this is your opportunity to say 'Cool to c u—let me know if u want to c me'. Clear texting gets clear answers. Boys are not mind-readers when it comes to interpreting your text—in fact, no one is. But with boys in particular you need to be as straightforward as possible when it comes to texting.

'Talk to boys on both Facebook and face to face. Because in real life I talk to boys at school and Facebook is for other friends at other schools.'—*Ami, age 13*

The downside to e-talk

While technology gives you an easy way to keep in touch, there are also some downsides to consider.

(Mis-)interpreting texts

Saying things electronically can take out a lot of the real meaning, the feeling, the essence of what you really mean. Receiving a message like, 'Soz cant make it' could be read as rejection and create the feeling in you that the boy doesn't really like you anymore, when it could simply mean his parents won't let him go out and he doesn't want to tell you that because he's embarrassed. His brief 'Soz cant make it' needs to be clarified with a simple 'Why' if you feel the response is strange and doesn't fit with what you expected. With limited credit in your mobile account, a phone call to try and work out the reason may not be affordable, leaving you feeling a bit mixed up about how he feels towards you, especially if it was a big event. So ask him face to face, 'I was disappointed you couldn't make it, are you okay?'

On the other hand, a short text back from you to that cute boy you just met that says 'c u round' may make him feel you are totally not interested, and may leave you wondering what happened when you don't hear from him again. Texting, the new shorthand for talking, is always up for (mis-)interpretation, and often you will hear girls trying to work out what his last text really meant, or working through the dramas of not getting a text back when you definitely expected to get a response straightaway. Girls, be clear in a text! 'Yes, let's catch up soon—I'd like that. Call me' rather than 'c u round'.

Going public

Technology, the underground playground for girls to get to know boys and for boys to get to know girls, is such an easy way to get to know each other when you are still living at home under your parents' roof. But, be warned, your messages may go public and be forwarded on and on and on. So be careful what you write!

Online traps

Whether it be Twitter, Facebook, My Space or mobiles, there may be some traps that you need to watch out for. Keep your electronic messages simple and straight to the point, think before you hit the send button, and definitely say nothing you will live to regret.

Do's and Don'ts

- Remember to guard your privacy and not reveal too much detail about yourself, particularly personal stuff like which boy you like.
- Never lie (or even tell white lies) about your identity or say anything you will regret.
- It's always a good idea, if you are really upset and want to send an angry email, to wait 24 hours before you send it. THINK AND TALK TO SOMEONE BEFORE YOU SEND. The same goes with texting; it's too easy to say things you will regret 24 hours later. Feelings pass, they just take time.
- Pictures—don't post them or send them. Again, they may be forwarded on, and you may one day regret that you sent them. And, in particular, don't send your private pictures.

'I prefer talking to boys one-to-one rather than on my mobile because it gets the most out of your relationship. I hate texting. Boys can't hide who they are when I am with them face to face and it allows me to understand them more.'—*Olivia, age 18*

Factoid:
One in three teens surveyed by Teenage Research Unlimited, aged 13–18, say they are text messaged 10, 20, 30 times an hour by a partner inquiring where they are, what they're doing, or who they're with. Furthermore, 82 per cent of parents whose teens were emailed or texted 30 times per hour were unaware this was happening.

Hooking up online

Face-to-face talking time is important as being in each other's physical presence helps you to work out if he is going to be special to you. Yet, for some of you, it may be easier to talk to boys online rather than on public transport, at school or out at sports events, or wherever you find the type of boys you are attracted to.

Would you connect online with a boy you haven't met? This is a question you will be faced with, and I guess the rule I take with my own Facebook site is, I try and only include friends that I actually talk to on a regular basis, not just once in a blue moon or because they are a friend of a friend who wants to know me. This is not because I want to be exclusive—not at all. Rather, I know that my Facebook site is a reflection of me and once stuff goes up it's pretty near impossible to get it down.

Google: boys

Did you know that 'boys' isn't the most googled word in the universe? In fact, the two words most frequently googled are 'God' and 'sex'. Interesting, as some would say that God is the mystery of life, whereas sex is the way we create life. Exploring these words is one of the main reasons I believe we have been put here on earth! That is, to procreate—which means to reproduce or make life—as well as to try, in some humble way, to understand the higher purpose of why we are here. However, YouTube and Google certainly give us another way to find answers to our searches, especially when it comes to boys, so I had to have a look myself to see what I could find.

My search results were endless, but I did find some good questions to ask that will possibly be useful in helping you to get to know that boy. The internet is full of advice on what to ask, but just be prepared for the possibility that, whatever you do ask him, he may very well turn the question around and ask for your opinion, your answer.

Fun questions to ask your boyfriend

Before you get into the heavy stuff—when your relationship is pretty fresh and you're not quite serious—it's nice to get to know the silly basics of what makes that boy tick. What's his favourite colour? Which food does he absolutely despise? Can he beat you in a game of Monopoly?

Here are some fun questions to ask that boy:

- What's your favourite colour?
- Favourite board game?
- Describe yourself in a single word.
- Describe me in a single word.
- Would you go dress shopping or shoe shopping with me?
- Another girl hits on you in front of me. How would you handle it?
- What about if I wasn't there?
- What is your favourite body part?
- What song reminds you of me?
- Do you think we've met before in a previous life?

The serious stuff

Once things start looking like they're getting serious—or physical (or both)—it's a good time to start asking the more personal questions. If you're inexperienced at the 'girl talking to boy thang' or you're pretty shy when it comes to asking potentially awkward or embarrassing personal questions, it may be incredibly intimidating to dive right into a conversation of this sort. However, there are reasons you should:

Protect your heart. By the way he answers your questions, you may determine he's a little bit of a heartbreaker. Is he in it for the long run or are you a fling for him? Does he feel as strongly about you as you do about him? You don't even have to have a 'So ... where is this relationship going?' talk with him (that tends to scare boys off sometimes!) to find out what you need to know. How did his last relationship end? Are he and his exes still able to be friends?

Protect your health. As far as your health goes, you need to know how many girls he's been with (or at least whether he used protection every time), if he's been tested for STIs (sexually transmitted infections), and how many times he put himself at risk of getting an STI by not using protection.

By asking the heavy questions, you can see how comfortable you really feel with this boy and how well you two discuss uncomfortable topics. Being able to talk about anything is a sign that a relationship has a strong foundation.

To text or not to text ...

If you are the 'writer' rather than the 'face to face' girl, and can say in writing what you can't say in words because of nerves or because you are worried about putting your true feelings on the line, the electronic era can work for you. But remember, nothing will replace that face-to-face time of talking in person, that special time when you can actually look at each other and see the expression on his face and his body language—the sparks between you. And remember, there is nothing like a good old-fashioned handwritten note on your favourite stationery that you can slip into his hand to tell him how you really feel!

GETTING CONNECTED

12
Is he 4 me?

Attraction signals

There is no exact prescription of what a girl must do to get that boy's attention, but there are a lot of girls spending a lot of time fixing up their outsides, their looks, to make themselves sparkle in case he walks by. Manicures, hair, makeup and clothes all can work to an extent, but what's much more important is the girl inside the dress—that's you! And if you want him to notice you, you have to believe that you are worthy of that boy's attention!

Be careful, when you least expect it and are simply doing your 'thang' he will come walking across the room, through the crowd and come right up next to you and ask you for the first date. He may catch you off guard, like you were not expecting this boy to ever ask you out. But be willing to meet up with him, you never know, he might be the one who eventually becomes more than just a friend.

How will you know if he feels the same way as you? He will let you know if he is still interested by asking you out again, sending you a text or always turning up where he knows you will be. If you don't see him straightaway, it doesn't mean he is not interested in you. It may just be that he's not practised at doing the girl–boy thang. GIVE THIS BOY TIME!

You feel you can trust him when
you talk about yourself.

Getting comfortable

Think about what it is that makes you feel comfortable when you meet anyone for the first time, and the type of questions that help you unlock the important things about you. Start exploring what he does, what he likes doing, what his favourite colour is, what he gets into, what type of music he likes and what he doesn't like. Explore what he gets up to with his friends when girls are not around. Only then will you get the feeling that you are starting to get to know him. Try to keep things light and funny, and not too serious at first; wait a while before you ask him to help you save the world!

Whether this boy is tall, short, muscle-bound, freckly, dark, skinny or blond, a sports figure, movie star, singer, an Italian stallion or a leader, to you he stands tall, head and shoulders above everyone else. He speaks his own mind, he thinks for himself, he's quirky and he makes you laugh, and you feel you can trust him when you talk about yourself. Then simply just say yes! Have fun.

Nervous

Getting to know him can sometimes make you feel nervous and anxious, so remember to laugh! Watching a funny movie may help relieve some of that 'knot in the belly' feeling and help you to relax and really get to know him. And if you are super nervous, take a moment to breathe in and breathe out, or take a friend along with you so you can joke around and keep it light and have fun. Feeling comfortable and not pressured while talking to that boy or to boys in general is the goal, girls!

Be in the moment

When you're talking to that boy, be in the moment. And do not, no matter what, spend the entire time when you are getting ready to meet him thinking about what you are going to say when you are together. Knowing how to be present and notice what is happening around you wherever you are with that boy is your number one priority. The moment you start talking together, notice, pay attention to what is going on around you. If there is a puppy walking past on the side of the road, be present, be in the moment—take initiative and pat the little dog. It is the little things, the very normal day-to-day things that both of you have done independently for years growing up, that matter and will give you plenty to talk about.

If you go to the movies it's not always a great place to talk and actually get to know him. It is usually more about the movie, the action and just enjoying being in each other's company. Fun, silent times—saying nothing and just hanging out with each other and getting used to being in each other's energy—are very cool, too.

Set your boundaries

Know your absolute limits with that special boy you are talking to, especially when he wants to keep talking and get more serious with the physical attraction side of things. If his sexual attraction is too much for you to handle, speak up and let him know. Don't be afraid to set your own boundaries when talking to boys. 'I want to get to know you first!' And if it feels right and you are ready to get more involved, that is entirely up to you. But be aware of what you are getting yourself into. There's nothing wrong with a kiss, but remember your own personal rules around your sexuality. No

> Concentrate on doing what you love ... and the boy + friend will naturally come along. He will come and find you! Yes, I believe in attraction. Bees are quite capable of finding their flower.

one makes these up except you, and these are based on your values and beliefs.

And if you really feel you are not ready to be alone with this boy, there's nothing wrong with going out in a group or bringing a friend. Check that this is okay with him, especially if he has specifically asked to meet you alone. Maybe he can bring one of his friends along too, and the four of you can talk among yourselves just as friends. Simply be clear about what you need and what makes you comfortable.

If you are feeling sexually attracted to this boy—that tingly feeling inside when you think about him—it can get really difficult to talk. It can sometimes feel like you have lost the ability to think let alone speak! I know that may sound ridiculous, but if you're feeling sexual attraction, these feelings can seem extreme and overwhelming.

No kiss doesn't mean he doesn't want to see you again; it could simply mean he has as much sexual attraction for you that he acknowledges but doesn't want to act on right now. If you still feel there is some excitement in your belly and you want to get to know him, and it's positive, you feel good, I am certain he will say something like, 'Hey, what's up next week?'

*When I go out
on a date with a boy,
I would expect:*
'Chat to learn more about each
other for most of the date and then
maybe a kiss at the end to "seal the
deal" (i.e. to show you both want to
be more than friends).'
—Anastasia, *age 15*

Rejection

The boy you are attracted to says, 'I can't keep seeing you anymore—there is someone else', or for some reason he has lost interest. OMG! What do you do (besides wanting to kill him)? How do you deal with the rejection, right there and then? It happens every day, so if it happens to you, please trust that this boy was not right for you. Sure, say how upset, angry, hurt, sad or devastated you are—but walking away cleanly from any relationship is the best way. Try (without anger or resentment) to get clear about why he is ending the relationship and see if there is anything to repair. But if he has gone for another girl, it's probably better to let him go.

If he has the courtesy to talk about a break-up face to face, he gets some credit points for good character. (Some boys may not say anything, and then you just see them with someone else. Oh boy, that hurts a lot!) But remember to breathe as he is doing the rejecting and say to yourself, 'I am going to be much better off without this dude.'

Now, if this happens don't let me hear you say 'I hate all boys'. Any boy that has rejected you is not a representative of all boys in the whole wide world. Don't forget you may also find yourself in the position one day of having to say the exact same 'I'm sorry, this thang we've got going isn't working' line. If there is someone else, it may be less hurtful to not say anything about your new attraction, but if you feel it's necessary, go ahead. We are all human and have feelings, and sometimes we cannot control who it is we feel attracted to. However, rejection is tough for any of us

If you really liked a boy and wanted to hook up (make out) with him. What would you do?

'Move closer to him, watch for body signals, see if he moves away or whether he's looking at your lips, staring into your eyes, smiling in a slightly different way.'—*Annabelle, age 18*

'I would start flirting with him, or talk to him a lot (e.g. text, internet).'—*Rani, age 14*

'See if they start flirting first.' —*Cassie, age 14*

'Lots of touching (subtle) and make heaps of eye contact— body language is everything.' —*Alicia, age 15*

'Just let them come to you but make an impression in front of him.'—*Ting, age 14* to deal with. So if you're the one doing the rejecting, be kind, be gentle. It hurts.

Timing is also important. If this boy you don't want to see anymore has got a really important exam the next day, it might be thoughtful to wait a day or two before you end things.

And before you feel you need to end a relationship or say no to an invitation to get to know 'that boy', be sure that's exactly what you want. If you can't feel in your gut what to do, then run it by your six pack of friends that help you with your 'girl talking to boy thang'.

Infatuation

Throwing yourself at any boy is not a good look, but it can happen. Some girls just can't take no for an answer and will do absolutely anything to get that boy's attention. This kind of action usually says more about you than the boy or the rock star or whoever it is that you are head over heels in love with and talking about 24/7. Infatuation can actually come from a place of very low self-worth and respect for oneself. Be careful, especially if your thinking is only about him; don't start following him or you may be asked to stop. No stalking boys allowed! You've got much better things to do with your time. If you feel fantabulous about you, infatuation doesn't generally get a look-in.

Not getting his attention, checklist

He just doesn't notice your 'vibe' that you really like him, and nothing you have tried is working. How does this make you feel? Do you find yourself doing any of these things when a boy just can't return your smile or doesn't reply to your texts? Are you:

1. Playing a lot of music, but also getting upset when you hear certain songs that remind you he is just not that in 2 u?
2. Not hungry or starting to eat way too much?
3. Calling his friends to really just find out about him?
4. Still sending texts and hoping you get a reply?
5. Checking your online networks all the time just in case he got your message?
6. Feeling depressed?
7. Wanting to go hang out where you know he will be?
8. Thinking about what you 'should have said' to get his attention?

The key right here, if you are experiencing any of these feelings or thoughts, is to understand it is normal to feel disappointed, angry or let down, especially about boys. Once you have acknowledged your frustrations about 'that boy' you can get rid of him in some type of healthy ceremony, such as journaling or sharing with a trusted adult or friend—someone who is knowledgeable enough to give you some honest feedback about you.

13
Six talk
times

My personal theory is that six talk times with that boy who is really interested in talking to you will give you enough time after you initially meet this boy to start listening to your gut feeling to work out whether or not he is right for you. Getting to know each other—checking out his likes and dislikes, his friends, and him checking out yours—may take more time than this, but **six talk times** is a good guide to find out what you have in common and whether or not the two of you will connect as more than just friends.

Talk time 1

The first official time you get to really talk to that boy it's exciting but it can also be be a bit uncomfortable as there is a lot to find out about this boy, and you may not be really sure if you like him. You know you like the way he looks and his reputation, but you don't really know him. And yes of course you feel a zing in your body (that is essential); a physical attraction and a willingness to get to C IN 2 him are unequivocally important. That means, one without the other is probably not going to work. But many of you will lose all sensibility when you enter into the space of his good looks without getting to know him first.

Be warned: Getting to know him on a first talk time will end up in a place you may not be prepared for or want to go if you let yourself enter into a dimly lit comfortable space. When your hormones kick in and the happy feelings start jumping around in your body if he kisses you straightaway, it's truly very hard to stop. Once you get started, you may not have the language to say, 'Stop, I am not ready for this.' There are plenty of girls who have got into trouble right from the word go. And there are also lots of girls who are able to voice this, after a very nice kiss: 'That's enough for now.' Which, by the way, will keep him interested if he is meant to be the one you will continue to get to know.

Talk times 2, 3 and 4

The next three times you meet that boy you think you like, try and go to different places, with friends and without. Keep it light and fun and make certain you keep doing the things that are important in your life. (This will be hard because when you are getting to know this boy, he will start to consume a lot of your thinking time.) Why not include night-time venues as well as daytime places so you are surrounded by a range of different things to talk about?

You may think you need to make the first move (you know, holding hands, that kiss, hooking up), but a first move can be as simple as a smile; it doesn't have to be anything outrageous that makes you feel uncomfortable.

(This will depend, of course, on whether you are allowed out at night and if your parents are okay with you seeing a boy.) Meeting up for lunch near the beach or going to a gathering with a group of school friends could all work to get to know him, and will ensure you're in a place where you feel safe.

During this time, you may have the extraordinarily lush experience of 'hooking up', once upon a time also known as 'pashing off' (kissing for a long time). Feeling tingly all over can feel amazing but keep your cool and keep him at a safe (sexual) distance until you are absolutely certain you want to share your intimacy with this boy! Intimacy definitely needs to be a mutually shared feeling by both you and that boy glued to your lips!

Talk times 5 and 6

By this stage you might have the confidence to ask him to come and watch you play sport on Saturday or you may be asked to go and watch him. You might even meet the family! If you get to this stage you can trust that his feelings are genuine and he is very comfortable with just getting to know you. He is what I would call very much IN 2 U. Talking time with this boy is the window you need to get to know him and for him to get to know who you are too.

There is no need to rush this talk time, the dates. Keep letting him call you during this time! I know this can be difficult, especially if a few days go past without a text, a call, a hello or some type of electronic message. No one can really prepare you for all the events that will occur when you start going out with a boy that you really like. Some girls will get very anxious when the mobile doesn't ring and there will be others that can simply say, 'Whatever, I'll see him whenever', and keep getting on with their lives. Knowing in their gut if he is the right boy, things will work out naturally.

When deep feelings of excitement and happiness start to bubble to the surface just thinking about him, and things don't work out the way you thought they would—that is, you have lost interest, or you both decide you would rather just remain friends—you will be very grateful that you have spent the time getting to know him first and saved your intimacy for that boy who just hasn't found you yet!

Making time to actually get together and talk face to face with boys can often be tricky. With school, sports, extracurricular activities and family commitments, there isn't always a lot of time left to talk to boys. School holidays can make things a little easier … But, of course, we all know where there is a will to talk that boys find a way.

Where to go to talk

It takes **confidence** and **patience** to attract the boy most naturally suited to you, and when he is standing right there in front of you asking you what you like doing and where you would like to go out, you'll need to be prepared. Open up opportunities that will create a lot of fun and a lot of talking time. Here are some ideas to get you started:

- Fun parks. Must have a Ferris wheel.
- Walk and talk! Don't be afraid of Mother Nature, she will give you plenty to talk about.
- Share a meal together.
- Favourite sport—get tickets to a game.
- Art shows or live bands.
- Music—dance.

It is kind of romantic, that first kiss, first hug, first date. But it can also be a big let-down sometimes, so ensure it is the best experience you can possibly make it because your memory of your first kiss will be with you all your life!

The next step

Once he gets to know you he might start to invite you into his group of friends and talk about you a lot (in a good way), or he may even invite you to his home to meet his mum or dad (OMG! That's big). Then there are those formal occasions, like dances—all that type of fun is going to give you plenty of opportunity to see how that boy shows you he is attracted to you.

Meeting his friends can feel a bit scary sometimes, but remember, while they are checking you out, you can do the same and get to know the type of people he chooses to hang out with. If he has brought you into his circle, it's because he wants you to get to know him more. Don't be over-paranoid or scared, just be the confident girl he was attracted to—that's you!

If he invites you to meet his parents, in his own way he is helping you get to know him more intimately. Enjoy it and have fun! Food is really important in a lot of cultures, and sharing a meal with his family can be a really important step in 'getting to know each other'.

14

Connecting
with 'me'

Connecting with yourself is all about learning how to plug into the power supply that is going to keep you feeling fit each and every day. This does not have to be complex, but it will require you to find a certain amount of balance in all areas of your life. That is, your school life, your social life, your family life, your 'me' time.

If you want to trust yourself and be the confident young woman who knows how to trust her own gut feeling, then finding balance in all areas of your life is really important. We make hundreds of decisions every minute of the day, and the older you get the more complex some of these decisions will become. Knowing what you want, what makes you happy and what you need will become more and more important every year. Especially when it comes to all those beautiful boys!

No one can make decisions about your life better than you, but if you are disconnected from yourself—that is, not looking after you—you may end up making bad choices that compromise the girl you want to be.

Finding the connections that are going to make you feel on top is not easy. There are so many distractions that will come along to take your time away from taking care of yourself. There are always

> Try this … Sit still and start to breathe in and out.
> Be still and connect with you. Ask yourself the
> question: 'Is this boy good for me?'

so many more pleasurable things to do than taking care of our basic needs daily. However, once you've got your daily rituals in place, they can be easy and a non-negotiable part of your life. Would you ever not recharge your mobile? No—you wouldn't want to miss his text or his call. So ask yourself, would you consider not connecting with yourself? The habit of recharging you every day is what will make you stand out!

Daily connections

Every night before you go to sleep, try and go over the day in your mind, reflecting on the highlights and the lowlights. It's usually been a good day if you can close your eyes and go to sleep as soon as your head hits the pillow. However, if you find yourself tossing and turning and your mind focusing on unresolved issues from the day, it's probably a good sign that you need to make things right as soon as you can. If anything is bugging you, make a mental note not to hold on to it, and aim to find someone to talk to the next day who can help you make sense of your part in the drama.

Try this … Sit still and start to breathe in and out. Be still and connect with you. Ask yourself a question: 'Is this boy good for me?'

Listen and wait for the answer from
within you to come into your mind.

Listen and wait for the answer from within you to come into your mind. If that small, quiet voice says, 'talk to him', then trust your judgement and don't be afraid to get to know him. Equally, if you get a sense that talking to him is not right for you right now, trust your gut reaction.

There is nothing worse than feeling indecisive when it comes to thinking about that boy; not being able to make up your mind can really do your head in! Sometimes you may find you want to talk to that boy, but you know in your gut that it's all wrong for you. If you can listen to yourself in this instance, wow! That's very mature thinking.

Daily 'neglections'

Connecting with yourself is simple once you know how, but lots of us neglect ourselves and don't even realise we are doing this. We may eat food on the run, not get enough sleep, fail to make the time to exercise or keep forgetting about the importance of drinking enough water. Some of us find we are so busy running around helping everyone else stay on top of their problems that we neglect to do the things that are necessary for ourselves.

Meditation

Each morning, I listen to a meditation application I have downloaded onto my iPhone. All I have to do is touch a button and choose a five-, ten-, 15-, or 20-minute breathing exercise. The voice comes on and guides me all the way, I don't have to do anything except breathe and focus on being right in the minute. Why do it? It's healthy for my mind. Just like I wouldn't start the day without taking a few minutes to brush my teeth to keep them clean, white and healthy, the breathing exercise keeps my spirit awake, fresh and sparkly. If you learn how to meditate every day it will make you feel brilliant. Meditation takes practice, and daily discipline, even if it's for five minutes, is better than nothing. It is a very powerful tool that could be your secret weapon when it comes to boys. Google 'breathing' and 'meditation'. I dare you to try it!

Affirmation: I am important, the daily things I do for myself keep me fit mentally, physically and emotionally.

When I want to stay connected to me when I am thinking about that boy 24/7? 'Look in the mirror and go through the positive things about me.' —*Lauren, age 14*

Reality check

Don't you just wish you had that personal trainer every day to wake you up, get you to the gym, sit with you while you meditate, pour you your eight glasses of water and make certain you have those three all-important meals, and then inspire you to get those eight hours of beauty sleep? I know—stop dreaming, who are we kidding? Can you believe that there are some girls who can do this already, all by themselves? And yes, then there is the majority of us that will always need help to be reminded to connect and take care of ourselves. Start with working out whether you are an owl or a fowl (i.e. a night bird or a morning bird), because this helps you to develop a routine that will work for you. And from this point, start planning some basic routines that will keep your body, heart, mind and soul fit.

My very own six pack

It's so easy to spend all day every day wishing you were someone you're not. This is not a good look and can eventually eat you up inside. You'll never hear your own gut feeling (or that small voice within you) about anything if you continually want to be

> Your heart will not get it wrong; your little voice
> inside, your gut feeling, will not let you down.

someone other than who you are. So how do we connect better with ourselves?

We are all used to spending some time talking to our friends, our mums and flicking through those glossy magazines to help us connect with who we are, but who are the six people in your world who you would dare to bare your soul to? Who is your **six pack**, the six people who help you stick to your gut feeling? Are they: older cousins; friends; best friends; teachers; sisters; brothers; boys as friends; family; your mum?

Connecting with what we want for ourselves can work in a number of ways. The more traditional way to work out if we are going to say 'yes' to the boy who has asked us to the school formal is to maybe ask your group or your best friend what they think. The more unconventional way would be to listen to yourself, to sit still and ask, do I really want to go to my formal with 'that boy', and then listen to the voice in your heart. Your heart will not get it wrong; your little voice inside, your gut feeling, will not let you down.

Your best friends

Opening up to your girlfriends or your best friend can help you get clearer when it comes to thinking about what's right for you when talking to boys. Asking what your friends think is important, but not more important than what you think yourself. Be prepared that sometimes your girlfriends may water down your enthusiasm for how you feel about that boy, and that their values might be very different to yours on a whole range of do's and don'ts when it comes to boys.

Your friends may not feel he is the right one for you; they might think, for example, that he is not good enough. He may be too flirty with all the girls and not conscious of how that will make you feel, and your friends don't want to see you get hurt.

Sure, we all talk to our girlfriends, but in the end it all comes back to you and what you think. That's why it's important to know how to trust your own gut feeling, especially when it comes to boys.

Wanted: One boy—down to earth; nice muscles; gentle and kind; cares a lot; energetic; funny; talks to girls nicely; likes sports; hot body; is able to talk to girls with confidence; cute; adorable; likes nothing illegal; family-friendly; funny; smart; sensitive; outgoing; good hairstyle; and calls you beautiful because you are, even when you're having a bad hair day.

Not wanted: Self-centred; lies about his freedom and where he is going; only talks to girls who are flirty and outgoing; jealous, but says it's cause he cares; doesn't keep a good body; can be nice, but most of the time he's a gronk (idiot).

15
Talking 2
parents

You will not be the first or the last girl to have an argument with your parents about being allowed to go out and talk to boys, or go on a date with that special boy, or just go out to some party with all your friends. The key here is to find the middle ground that will give you a reasonable voice to express what your heart desires to your parents while respecting their wishes for you. It is all in the way you ask!

OMG, my parents!

The reality for a lot of girls is that they feel they can't talk to their parents about boys. It's hard enough just getting comfortable talking with a boy at the start, let alone talking about him to your parents. While some girls' parents are very cool with the whole idea of being the bouncing board for the ups and downs about talking to boys, these parents often find they are not just talking to their own daughters, but that the information they are passing on is being shared among their daughter's friends. While their wisdom can be gold, sometimes, in the process of passing the message down the line, the original meaning can become lost in translation. That's why it is really important to have someone from the adult world to talk to yourself just about you!

'In my culture [Sudan] teenagers are not allowed to have sex until married and you cannot get married to a guy who's younger than you. He must be 5–6 years older than you. It's also weird to talk to your mum about boys and feelings and sex in my culture because your mum would start getting worried and insecure about you and think you're going to have sex or get wasted at the age of 13–19.'—*Margaret, age 16*

Different values

Parents, belief systems about their (little girl) daughter talking to boys come in all shapes and sizes, and these ideas all seem to come with their own rule book. Some are very strict, loud, annoying and weird (unfair) when it comes to talking to boys. Some parents are very stern and have certain disciplines in their cultural and religious systems when it comes to the way their daughters should talk to boys. And some parents will have no rules at all.

In the end, you may find your parents just don't like the boy you choose to talk to. Maybe they think he is not good for you, that he's the 'bad boy' and will cause you trouble. It's your job, then, to convince them otherwise, but if there are solid reasons for them to believe he is not good for their little girl—that's you—then you can hardly blame them for only wanting the best for you.

How to win

No one escapes having (heated talks) fights with their parents. What you want to do and what they will let you do are often two completely different things, and that might feel very unfair at the time, especially if all your friends are allowed to do what you believe you should be able to do to! Especially just going out so you can meet boys!

The key here is, if you want your parents to hear what you are saying, definitely don't start mentioning what all your friends are allowed to do. That will clearly not work because their only concern is you, not your friends. And their values about going out may be very different to your friends'. Just give them all the facts about where you want to go, who with and who is going to be there. This will be a great start to helping your parents feel reassured that you will be safe. And if there are going to be boys there, or that 'special boy to you', be clear about that too.

If it looks like you are not going to get your own way, throwing a tantrum, slamming a door or stamping your foot will probably not help things along; rather, it may take you back to a big, fat, simple 'No, you can't go.' If you do get a 'No' and you start kicking and screaming, you have probably just made things worse for yourself, giving you not much room to come back with a Plan B. So, let's say Plan B worked and you are allowed to go out, but you have to be home early. 'What's the point of going?' you say! You are about to argue that everyone else can stay out till later, and then you quickly remember that tactic won't work. Just let your parents know enough detail about where you are going and who with so that everyone is in the loop, just in case something horrible does happen and they need to find you.

16
Boy troubles

His way or your way?

There is a girl at your school who keeps flirting with your boyfriend. He can't see anything wrong with her friendliness, but you certainly can. You become very jealous and start arguing with him to get him to stop talking to her. He says no. You cry. You become agitated and angry, and storm off. You're consumed by jealousy and it threatens to destroy your trust in this boy. And an argument starts; he is confused because he can't see anything wrong with her friendliness and believes he is doing nothing wrong. What do you do?

When you have a disagreement with that boy you like, do you sit down and talk it out? Do you talk to a friend? Do you stop talking and give him the silent treatment, and then, when you have settled down, talk over the trouble? Do you argue back? Do you scream and shout? Don't know what to do?

Boy troubles are the kinds of things we all wish happened to everyone else, right? Fighting, arguing, not getting along; it's enough to put a big knot in your stomach and can cause lots of unnecessary heartache.

If you do fight, have a way of finishing
the argument and moving on.

What you believe and what you want are not always the same
as what the boy you are talking to will want, and this can cause
lots of trouble. Who will get their own way? Or can you come
to a solution that works for both of you? 'Do you really have to
smoke?' you keep asking until it becomes an issue that you just
cannot agree on. What do you do?

The bright side to most conflicts and arguments is that, if you
really want to sort them out, they are generally resolvable. The
key here is being willing to talk, but you may need help to do this,
especially if you grew up in a home where lots of arguments was
or is the 'norm'.

Agree to disagree

On a trip to Brazil a few years ago I watched a television host on
a talk-back show interview a young teenage couple. They could
not agree on a solution to their problem and were arguing it out
on national television. The problem being discussed was that the
Brazilian boy followed the soccer religiously and had tickets to the
finals—his team was playing and nothing was going to stop him from
attending, not even the funeral of his girlfriend's grandmother. Both

sides of the argument had their valid points, and being on national television gave the other participants on the show an opportunity to voice their support for or against the issues raised. Potentially, there could have been a show-down fight, but because the couple had some neutral ground on which they could each express their emotions of anger, disappointment, disapproval and rage, they were both able to win. He went to the soccer, she went to the funeral.

I know we all can't go on national television to sort out our troubles, but we can create a similarly neutral environment with a counsellor or an adult friend if we really need help.

Fixing the trouble

Edward de Bono, a favourite thinker and philosopher of mine, recommends, once we are in a 'committed' relationship as girlfriend and boyfriend, that every seven years we consider renewing the reasons why we are still talking with that same boy. Not a bad idea—it would certainly keep things very fresh! While I can't imagine any of you thinking you will still be with the boy you are with today for another seven years (some may disagree here— sorry, girls!), I think it's a useful concept, nonetheless, to keep the boyfriend–girlfriend thing fresh by renewing the reasons every so often that we were attracted to each other in the first place.

It would be a good idea, if you do fight, to have a way of finishing the argument and moving on, rather than keep dragging the chain along from every fight you ever have and allowing it to affect your future together.

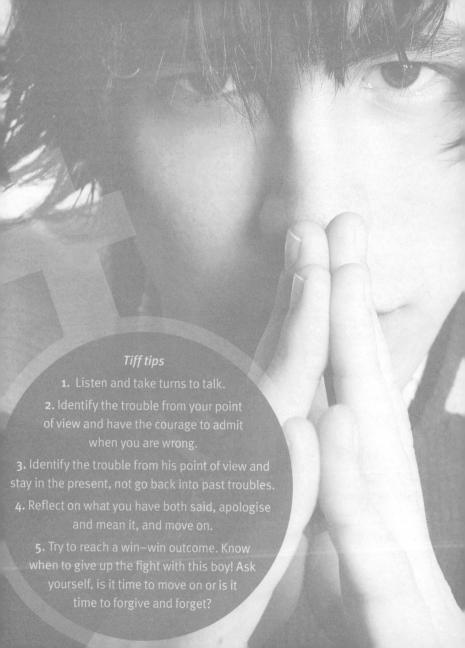

Tiff tips

1. Listen and take turns to talk.

2. Identify the trouble from your point of view and have the courage to admit when you are wrong.

3. Identify the trouble from his point of view and stay in the present, not go back into past troubles.

4. Reflect on what you have both said, apologise and mean it, and move on.

5. Try to reach a win–win outcome. Know when to give up the fight with this boy! Ask yourself, is it time to move on or is it time to forgive and forget?

Trouble with a capital T: Bad boys

Every girl knows at least one 'bad boy'. This is the type of boy that is usually hot and very smooth when it comes to talking to girls, but wants to push life to its limits and take you with him for the ride. He is the one who asks you to go where you have not yet been; the one you may decide to take some risks with that you may live to regret. Some of these bad boys have what seems like 'animal magnetism', an attraction that feels impossible to resist. But it takes two. A bad boy alone can only cause trouble for himself, but add yourself to the equation, and yes, then there is double trouble.

This is the time to tap into your own values, your own self-respect and the hopes you have for yourself around your body, heart, mind and soul. Choosing the bad boy is just that, a choice. Only you can make this decision. Definitely know what you want before you start talking to that bad boy!

'If I became sexually active before I was emotionally ready I may feel regret and that all the boy wanted was my body, not all of me. Then my self-esteem would drop and I would feel completely guilty.'—*Jenna, age 17*

'I wouldn't want her to but I can't stop her, as long as she is SMART ABOUT IT (uses protection).'—*Portia, age 17*

'I want my daughter (in the future) to wait for the right guy and not race into the future.'—*Trish, age 14*

'Choosing Mr Cool' by Fern Christian
(A personal story about choosing the bad boy)

When I was in Year 8 I was on the Honour Roll at school, but at age 15, in Year 9, things weren't too happy at home and I decided to hang out with a different crowd, to make some 'cool' friends. These friends liked to hang out at night, they skipped school, drank beer, smoked pot and sometimes did other drugs. They were pretty cool in my eyes.

It was a time when I thought I had all the answers. I wouldn't listen to anyone. The stricter my mother was, the more I went ahead and did what I wanted. I never had a father. That year I lost my virginity to my first boyfriend. My second boyfriend slapped me one day when I did something to make him angry, and afterwards he said he was sorry and it would never happen again. I believed him.

At age 16, I became pregnant to my second boyfriend, and we decided to marry. I never considered abortion; it wasn't legal at the time, but I had heard that you could get one if you really tried. I wouldn't give him up for adoption either. I had a strong love for my baby and wanted him very much.

I wasn't afraid of missing much at school because I hadn't been a part of school life for quite a while, although I did regret missing the senior formal. I was ready to leave school and ready to leave home.

Giving birth at 17 was a happy experience; my son was born and I loved him so much, but soon afterwards the physical abuse became worse. There was a cycle of me getting beaten, both of us crying, and then he'd promise never to do it again. But there was always a next time. My 17-year-old husband was smoking pot every day and lying to me all the time. He'd work all day and then disappear nearly every night. After one beating, my baby and I went to my mother's house, and the next day she sent me back to him. I guess she had gotten used to not having me around.

One night we had a fight and I finally decided to fight back. That surprised him and he left. It was a small victory because he came back the next day and punched me so hard in the eye that my head flew back into the glass in the door. My eye swelled so much, so fast, that it stuck out like you see in a cartoon. I had glass in my head and the white of my eye went bright red.

I went to a lawyer to file for divorce. The lawyer took a photo of me with my black eye and he showed it to the judge at the hearing. My husband denied hitting me but no one believed him. I was granted child support of $35 a week but I never received any of it.

By 18, I was a single mother working full time and trying to raise my son. I can't say that it wasn't difficult and we did have our share of issues over time, but we always loved each other. I had to be strong because there was no one around to rescue me.

High school can be difficult but it can also be fun. Keep friends who are the kinds of people that you want to be; choose wisely. Be good to yourself and value yourself highly. If your friends are doing drugs, make new friends.

Take the time to be young because the years ahead will be full of responsibility. The best way to never have to make a decision about a pregnancy is to not get pregnant in the first place! Be in charge and be happy!

It's your choice

There are laws in every country around the world on the legal age that is required for sexual intercourse. But while the laws are there to protect us, the only one who can really do that is you. It may have turned out that the 'hottie' you made a choice to be with, or the bad boy who all the girls wanted, wasn't actually your prince. Perhaps he meant more to you than you meant to him. If you fall pregnant there will be a long-term effect on your life choices. We only get one life, and the decisions we make every day determine the script for that life. The life lessons you learn talking to boys may be the lessons you teach to your own daughter one day. Remember, if you believe that your Mr Darcy will find you he probably will. The power of our thinking is amazing.

In the back of this book there are a number of Google searches that may help you. Make sure you don't wait too long to find answers to questions you just don't feel you can ask. Some girls really feel that they are alone and try to work out boy problems on their own, and it's not until they are in trouble that they seek advice. When we are young and talking to boys we can feel bullet-proof, but the sad part is there are lots of girls who will ignore their gut feelings when it comes to talking to those notorious bad boys.

Have confidence talking to boys

Being confident about your choices when talking to boys will require absolute belief in yourself and your abilities. Being able to articulate (speak) your truth and know what you want and don't want will definitely keep you on track to realise your fullest potential. You will be required, along the road of 'girl talking to boy', not to be afraid to admit when you have made mistakes and to be able to pick yourself up and shake off the dust. We can all learn from our experiences of pain and troubles. Trouble with boys, as unfortunate as it is, is often a great teacher and a healer. Remember, it can be a lipstick jungle out there talking to boys, so take care and remember to keep your emergency lip balm handy.

'No one really listens to all that information you get about safe sex, they don't think it's going to be them!'—*Anastasia, age 18*

1. Attraction: Boy naturally finds me. I am happy in my life; he met me doing something I love? Or Distraction: I find boy. He makes me feel good about myself. I don't like me; he will make me feel better?

2. Am I confused about this boy or just infatuated by him? Or do I feel comfortable and excited about getting to know him?

3. Is he a paper tiger (just a hottie), or is he the boy who will talk to his parents about me and take time to get to know the girl I am? Does he just look good on the outside, or is he the type of boy that makes my heart sing and I know in my gut it feels right for me?

5. If I am in tears, fights and arguments rather than being happy, ask myself, do I really need this boy in my life? Is it time to move on?

4. Am I prepared to go on six dates to get to know this boy? If I am still unsure about him can I talk to my six pack of friends who I trust and know care for me?

6. Talking to this boy is packed with fun, excitement and respect. Am I prepared to let him know how special he is to me?

17
Love

What is love?

There are many girls who have come before us in search of the answers to this question, and many more will follow. Love is definitely nothing to be scared about, but there are plenty of people who fear love; they feel that it might require something of them they cannot give, but we all really do have the capacity to love and to be loved.

My personal view on love: Love is not awkward, nor is it going to compromise you. Love will not require you to do anything that does not feel right for you. We were created to love and to be loved, and it's the sexual urges that are within each of us that pull us out of ourselves to attract someone we can share that love with one day. Real love is a gift from yourself to another person. Love is not using someone for our own purposes. Love is not controlling another person, yet it requires us at times to show self-control of our natural healthy desires and attraction to boys.

Love is respectful.

Is love 4 ever?

Today, about one in three marriages and de facto relationships (a couple living together) end, and it's usually due to communication (talking) going all wrong, or perhaps the respect and trust in the relationship that was once so important has been lost. With those startling realities it makes sense that young people like yourself are questioning what love is all about when talking to boys.

Anna, age 17, said it's a bit confusing thinking about love when you are a teenager: 'Love is when you feel like you can't live without someone, and I think teenagers love each other but they are not in love; they love each other as people. Real love is like marriage, commitment. It's nice to think about it, but in reality so many people get divorced.'

'Give your hearts, but not into each other's keeping.
For only the hand of Life can contain your hearts.
And stand together yet not too near together:
For the pillars of the temple stand apart,
And the oak tree and the cypress grow not in each other's shadow.'

—An excerpt from The Prophet, 'On Marriage' by Khalil Gibran

Letters to my daughter

Imagine one day in the future, when you have found the boy who you can talk to so easily, the one you can't wait to see and who you can be your true self around, and you decide to go out. You become girlfriend and boyfriend. You start a relationship and are committed to each other. Now, fast forward and visualise you have been happily together for years and have an incredible 15-year-old daughter of your own. What would you say to her if she came to you, her mother, to ask what to do when it comes to that boy who has got her serious attention?

Dear future daughter,

My advice to you on talking to boys would have to be that you should not start talking to them until you totally respect yourself. There will be boys that you will meet who are only looking for one thing, but you need to be strong enough to not be the girl that gives in to them until you are sure it's the right choice.

Not everyone is like this though, so be patient and let love take its course. Don't rush into anything, do not feel pressured to keep up with what 'everyone else is doing' because eventually you will learn you are not 'everyone else' and half of these people won't be there for you when you need them as not everyone is true to their word.

Do not be a pushover, this will get you nowhere. Be sure to surround yourself with people you want to be like, ones that love you for who you are not what you do, for these are your greatest influences.

Of course you will make mistakes, and you may have many loves before the one you're happy with. Don't let movies or TV fool you into thinking love should be a particular way; it can be whatever you want it to be.

At the end of the day be sure the choices you make are what you wanted, because you never leave yourself, the decisions you make shape you to who you become and what you want to be.

Love mum :)

Indiah Jackson, age 16

18
Fairytale endings

One day you might find yourself sitting down to talk to your child about how you first started talking to boys, and whether or not your story will look like a fairytale or a series of unfortunate events is entirely up to the choices you start making during your teenage years. Who you allow to get to know you as your sweetheart is entirely your decision and will be a whole lot easier if you truly get being able to let him find you.

There is no better judge on boys than you. And if you are truly doing what you love and loving who you are (yes, that means your body too), don't be surprised if you look up from what you are passionately doing one day to see that the boy who feels so easy to talk to has just walked into your life!

Talking to your prince

It is a winterlicious night and you are curled up in front of the warm glow of an open fire with the boy (who has now become the man) you love, and he asks you to recall how you first got started talking to boys.

Your mind flashes back into the memory tapes of your early teens that, believe it or not, will one day in the not so distant

Is he the right boy for me?

future seem like forever ago. The amber glow of the fireplace stirs up the interest in the face of the man who has captured your attention, and your mind starts backtracking and flashing up all those colourful moments that recall the BIG questions about boys that you had back then.

What am I going to wear? Is he the right boy for me? Do I need to make the first move? How do I know he feels the same way as me? How do I let him get to know me and how do I get to know him? Why do I feel like marshmallow when he walks into the room? Could this be love? Does my bum look big in this? Do you think he's cute? Is he the one?

Then you remember, OMG—that book, *How to Talk to Boys*, that got me started talking to boys and changed my life. You treasured it, you read each single word twice just to make sure you didn't miss out on one iota of information—you even put this book in your cherished memory box so that one day you could even pass it on to your own daughter.

You related to the stories of what girls really want to talk to boys about and how they feel about themselves, and found out the important questions to ask to see if this boy is going to become more than just a friend. And, most importantly, you found out how to know if that boy you think is the 'right' boy is in fact the 'bad' boy. Thank heavens someone shared this vital information on how boys think. That's right, it was a non-negotiable must-read.

You stare back into your sweetheart's long gaze and take a deep breath and think, I wonder if he is ready to hear about the heartache, the tragic tricks, the trouble, the mistakes, the must do's that I went through talking to boys in my teens? And then you remember that he loves you unconditionally and you can talk to him about absolutely anything because you 'get it' with no single doubt in your head and your heart that you are in 2 him and he is in 2 u 2.

You snuggle deep into his strong caressing arms wrapped around your hips, and start to recall in your mind how simple the 'how' in talking to boys really was after you read *How to Talk to Boys*.

You finally got the true meaning of that word 'intimacy' (or 'in 2 me u c', as you used to like to say). There is no question that with that well-read dog-eared copy of HTTTB in your hot little hands, you now have the quintessentials in your life to attract a conversation 'talk time' with a boy that respects you doing the things you love 4 u.

However, 'in 2 me u c' now has a completely different meaning, and right here right now you don't want to spoil the moment, so you save the conversation by knowing in your heart that one of the ways not to talk to boys is to bring up the old flames you have talked to and loved in the past. Especially if this information is going to stop you being in the present in front of this cosy winter glow.

Instead of recapturing every single moment in your life that didn't work talking to boys—you break from his caress, run upstairs and get your well-worn, cherished copy of *How to Talk to Boys* and put it in his hands. He flicks to the double-page spread, 'in 2 me u c'.

You know deep in your heart that 'in 2 me u c thinking' changed the way you felt about yourself and the way you talked to boys ... and that the boys who read this book also had inside information into girls.

And yes, he eventually did take the book from your hands and started to read, and you did look into each other's eyes and make out! But I am not saying you both lived happily ever after, because that requires a commitment, an every single daily grind to keep a respectful connection. And no one has this crystal ball to ensure either of you will keep doing that every day, year in and year out, for ever and ever.

And if the time ever comes when you are in too much pain because your talking to boys thang is not working, remember to go back to this cute little book and read it again. Accept the things you can't change, take courage with the things you can, and have the wisdom to change whatever is necessary to keep your girl talkin' to boy thang happening. I do!

Resources

Google searches to further support concepts explored in this book:

Meditation; affirmations; Jean Piaget; Erik Erikson; Edward De Bono; VIA signature strengths; age of consent for sex; drinking changes your thinking;

Websites:
www.communicatekids.com
www.kidshelp.com.au

References:
Books sourced and read for inspiration during the research of this book:

Facing Love Addiction by Pia Mellody (Harper Collins, 2003).

He. Understanding Masculine Psychology by Robert A. Johnson (Harper Collins, 1989).

She. Understanding Feminine Psychology by Robert A. Johnson (Harper Collins, 1989).

We: Understand The Psychology of Romantic Love by Robert A. Johnson (Harper Collins, 1983).

Women's Bodies, Women's Wisdom by Dr Christiane Northrup (Bantam, 1998).

INDEX

First published in 2011

Copyright © text Dianne Todaro 2011
Copyright © concept Dianne Todaro 2011

Allen & Unwin
Sydney, Melbourne, Auckland, London

83 Alexander Street
Crows Nest NSW 2065
Australia
Phone: (61 2) 8425 0100
Fax: (61 2) 9906 2218
Email: info@allenandunwin.com
Web: www.allenandunwin.com

Cataloguing-in-Publication details are available
from the National Library of Australia
www.trove.nla.gov.au

ISBN 978 1 74237 438 3

Cover and internal design by Seymour Designs
Internal photography by iStockphoto
Printed in Australia by McPherson's Printing Group

10 9 8 7 6 5 4 3 2 1